ECONOMIC ISSUES, PROBLEMS AND PERSPECTIVES

DERIVATIVES REFORM AND REGULATION

ECONOMIC ISSUES, PROBLEMS AND PERSPECTIVES

Additional books in this series can be found on Nova's website under the Series tab.

Additional E-books in this series can be found on Nova's website under the E-books tab.

ECONOMIC ISSUES, PROBLEMS AND PERSPECTIVES

DERIVATIVES REFORM AND REGULATION

AIDAN B. LYNCH
EDITOR

Nova Science Publishers, Inc.
New York

Copyright © 2011 by Nova Science Publishers, Inc.

All rights reserved. No part of this book may be reproduced, stored in a retrieval system or transmitted in any form or by any means: electronic, electrostatic, magnetic, tape, mechanical photocopying, recording or otherwise without the written permission of the Publisher.

For permission to use material from this book please contact us:
Telephone 631-231-7269; Fax 631-231-8175
Web Site: http://www.novapublishers.com

NOTICE TO THE READER

The Publisher has taken reasonable care in the preparation of this book, but makes no expressed or implied warranty of any kind and assumes no responsibility for any errors or omissions. No liability is assumed for incidental or consequential damages in connection with or arising out of information contained in this book. The Publisher shall not be liable for any special, consequential, or exemplary damages resulting, in whole or in part, from the readers' use of, or reliance upon, this material. Any parts of this book based on government reports are so indicated and copyright is claimed for those parts to the extent applicable to compilations of such works.

Independent verification should be sought for any data, advice or recommendations contained in this book. In addition, no responsibility is assumed by the publisher for any injury and/or damage to persons or property arising from any methods, products, instructions, ideas or otherwise contained in this publication.

This publication is designed to provide accurate and authoritative information with regard to the subject matter covered herein. It is sold with the clear understanding that the Publisher is not engaged in rendering legal or any other professional services. If legal or any other expert assistance is required, the services of a competent person should be sought. FROM A DECLARATION OF PARTICIPANTS JOINTLY ADOPTED BY A COMMITTEE OF THE AMERICAN BAR ASSOCIATION AND A COMMITTEE OF PUBLISHERS.

Additional color graphics may be available in the e-book version of this book.

Library of Congress Cataloging-in-Publication Data

Derivatives reform and regulation / editor, Aidan B. Lynch.
 p. cm.
Includes index.
ISBN 978-1-61324-935-2 (hardcover)
 1. Derivative securities--United States. 2. Derivative securities--Law and legislation--United States. 3. Financial services industry--Law and legislation--United States. 4. Securities industry--Law and legislation--United States. I. Lynch, Aidan B.
 HG6024.U6D472 2011
 332.64'570973--dc23
                    2011018562

Published by Nova Science Publishers, Inc. † New York

CONTENTS

Preface		vii
Chapter 1	Key Issues in Derivatives Reform *Rena S. Miller*	1
Chapter 2	Derivatives Regulation in the 111th Congress *Mark Jickling and Rena S. Miller*	29
Chapter 3	Conflicts of Interest in Derivatives Clearing *Rena S. Miller*	75
Chapter 4	The Dodd-Frank Wall Street Reform and Consumer Protection Act: Title VII, Derivatives *Mark Jickling and Kathleen Ann Ruane*	99
Index		121

PREFACE

Financial derivatives allow users to manage or hedge business risks that arise from volatile commodity prices, interest rates, foreign currencies and a wide range of other variables. Derivatives also permit potentially risky speculation on future trends in those rates and prices. Derivatives markets are very large, measured in the hundreds of trillions of dollars, and they grew rapidly in the years before the recent financial crisis. The events of the crisis have sparked calls for fundamental reform. This book examines the key issues in derivatives reform and regulation; the conflicts of interest in derivatives clearing and the Dodd-Frank Wall Street Reform and Consumer Protection Act.

Chapter 1- Financial derivatives allow users to manage or hedge certain business risks that arise from volatile commodity prices, interest rates, foreign currencies, and a wide range of other variables. Derivatives also permit potentially risky speculation on future trends in those rates and prices. Derivatives markets are very large—measured in the hundreds of trillions of dollars—and they grew rapidly in the years before the recent financial crisis. The events of the crisis have sparked calls for fundamental reform.

Chapter 2- In the wake of the financial crisis and unusual oil price volatility, new attention was drawn to the regulation of derivatives—and particularly toward the unregulated over-the-counter (OTC) derivatives market. What regulatory changes, if any, would reduce risks to the financial system from derivatives trading? A number of bills were introduced in the 111th Congress, and several congressional committees have held hearings. The Dodd-Frank Wall Street Reform and Consumer Protection Act (P.L. 111-203) enacted a sweeping reform of derivatives trading and oversight and brought the unregulated OTC swaps market under the jurisdiction of federal regulators.

Chapter 3- The financial crisis implicated the over-the-counter (OTC) derivatives market as a source of systemic risk. In the wake of the crisis, lawmakers sought to reduce systemic risk to the financial system by regulating this market. One of the reforms that Congress introduced in the Dodd-Frank Act (P.L. 111-203) was mandatory clearing of OTC derivatives through clearinghouses, in an effort to remake the OTC market more in the image of the regulated futures exchanges. Clearinghouses require traders to put down cash or liquid assets, called margin, to cover potential losses and prevent any firm from building up a large uncapitalized exposure, as happened in the case of the American International Group (AIG). Clearinghouses thus limit the size of a cleared position based on a firm's ability to post margin to cover its potential losses.

Chapter 4- The financial crisis implicated the unregulated over-the-counter (OTC) derivatives market as a major source of systemic risk. A number of firms used derivatives to construct highly leveraged speculative positions, which generated enormous losses that threatened to bankrupt not only the firms themselves but also their creditors and trading partners. Hundreds of billions of dollars in government credit were needed to prevent such losses from cascading throughout the system. AIG was the best-known example, but by no means the only one.

In: Derivatives Reform and Regulation ISBN: 978-1-61324-935-2
Editor: Aidan B. Lynch © 2011 Nova Science Publishers, Inc.

Chapter 1

KEY ISSUES IN DERIVATIVES REFORM[*]

Rena S. Miller

SUMMARY

Financial derivatives allow users to manage or hedge certain business risks that arise from volatile commodity prices, interest rates, foreign currencies, and a wide range of other variables. Derivatives also permit potentially risky speculation on future trends in those rates and prices. Derivatives markets are very large—measured in the hundreds of trillions of dollars—and they grew rapidly in the years before the recent financial crisis. The events of the crisis have sparked calls for fundamental reform.

Derivatives are traded in two kinds of markets: on regulated exchanges and in an unregulated over-the-counter (OTC) market. During the crisis, the web of risk exposures arising from OTC derivatives contracts complicated the potential failures of major market participants like Bear Stearns, Lehman Brothers, and AIG. In deciding whether to provide federal support, regulators had to consider not only the direct impact of those firms failing, but also the effect of any failure on their derivatives counterparties. Because OTC derivatives are unregulated, little information was available about the extent and distribution of possible derivatives-related losses.

The OTC market is dominated by a few dozen large financial institutions who act as dealers. Before the crisis, the OTC dealer system

---

[*] This is an edited, reformatted and augmented version of a Congressional Research Service publication, CRS Report for Congress R40965, from www.crs.gov, dated June 22, 2010.

was viewed as robust, and as a means for dispersing risk throughout the financial system. The idea that OTC derivatives tend to promote financial stability has been challenged by the crisis, as many of the major dealers required infusions of capital from the government.

Derivatives reform legislation before Congress would require the OTC market to adopt some of the practices of the regulated exchange markets, which were able to cope with financial volatility in 2008 without government aid. A central theme of derivatives reform is requiring OTC contracts to be cleared by a central counterparty, or derivatives clearing organization. Clearinghouses remove the credit risk inherent in bilateral OTC contracts by guaranteeing payment on both sides of derivatives contracts. They impose initial margin (or collateral) requirements to cover potential losses initially. They further impose variation margin to cover any additional ongoing potential losses. The purpose of posting margin is to prevent a build-up of uncovered risk exposures like AIG's. Proponents of clearing argue that if AIG had had to post initial margin and variation margin on its trades in credit default swaps, it would likely have run out of money before its position became a systemic threat that resulted in costly government intervention.

Benefits of mandatory clearing include greater market transparency, as the clearinghouse monitors, records, and usually confirms trades. Clearing may reduce systemic risk, by mitigating the possibility of nonpayment by counterparties. There are also costs to clearing. Margin requirements impose cash demands on "end users" of derivatives, such as nonfinancial firms who used OTC contracts to hedge risk. H.R. 4173, as passed by the House, and Title VII of the same bill, as amended with text from S. 3217 and passed by the Senate on May 20, 2010, provide exemptions from mandatory clearing for certain categories of market participants. If exemptions are too broad, then systemic risks, as well as default risks to dealers and counterparties, may remain. The bills seek to balance the competing goals of reducing systemic risk and preserving end users' ability to hedge risks through derivatives, without causing those derivatives trades to become too costly. This report analyzes the issues of derivatives clearing and margin and end users, and it discusses the various legislative approaches to the end-user issue.

GENERAL BACKGROUND

Derivative contracts are an array of financial instruments with one feature in common: their value is linked to changes in some underlying variable, such as the price of a physical commodity, a stock index, or an interest rate. Derivatives contracts—futures contracts, options, and swaps[1]— gain or lose value as the underlying rates or prices change, even though the holder may not actually own the underlying asset.

Thousands of firms use derivatives to manage risk. For example, a firm can protect itself against increases in the price of a commodity that it uses in production by entering into a derivative contract that will gain value if the price of the commodity rises. A notable instance of this type of hedging strategy was Southwest Airlines' derivatives position that allowed it to buy jet fuel at a low fixed price in 2008 when energy prices reached record highs. When used to hedge risk, derivatives can protect businesses (and sometimes their customers as well) from unfavorable price shocks.

Others use derivatives to seek profits by betting on which way prices will move. Such speculators provide liquidity to the market—they assume the risks that hedgers wish to avoid. The combined trading activity of hedgers and speculators provides another public benefit: price discovery. By incorporating all known information and expectations about future prices, derivatives markets generate prices that often serve as a reference point for transactions in the underlying markets.

Although derivatives trading had its origins in agriculture, today most derivatives are linked to financial variables, such as interest rates, foreign exchange, stock prices and indices, and the creditworthiness of issuers of bonds. The market is measured in the hundreds of trillions of dollars, and billions of contracts are traded annually.

Derivatives have also played a part in the development of complex financial instruments, such as bonds backed by pools of other assets. They can be used to create "synthetic" securities— contracts structured to replicate the returns on individual securities or portfolios of stocks, bonds, or other derivatives. Although the basic concepts of derivative finance are neither new nor particularly difficult, much of the most sophisticated financial engineering of the past few decades has involved the construction of increasingly complex mathematical models of how markets move and how different financial variables interact. Derivatives trading is often a primary path through which such research reaches the marketplace.

Since 2000, growth in derivatives markets has been explosive (although the financial crisis has caused some retrenchment since 2008). Between 2000 and the end of 2008, the volume of derivatives contracts traded on exchanges,[2] such as futures exchanges, and the notional value of total contracts traded in the over-the-counter (OTC) market[3] grew by 475% and 522%, respectively. By contrast, during nearly unprecedented credit and housing booms, the respective value of corporate bonds and home mortgages outstanding grew by 95% and 115% over the same period.[4]

MARKET STRUCTURE AND REGULATION

Although the various types of derivatives are used for the same purposes—avoiding business risk, or hedging, and taking on risk in search of speculative profits—the instruments are traded on different types of markets. Futures contracts are traded on exchanges regulated by the Commodity Futures Trading Commission (CFTC); stock options on exchanges under the Securities and Exchange Commission (SEC); and swaps (and some options) are traded OTC, and they are not regulated by anyone.

Exchanges are centralized markets where all the buying interest comes together. Traders who want to buy, or take a long position (longs), interact with those who want to sell, or go short (shorts), and deals are made and prices reported throughout the day. In the OTC market, contracts are made bilaterally, typically between a dealer and an end user, and there is generally no requirement that the price, the terms, or even the existence of the contract be disclosed to a regulator or to the public.

Derivatives can be volatile contracts, and the normal expectation is that there will be big gains and big losses among traders. As a result, there is a problem of market design. How do the longs know that the shorts will be able to meet their obligations, and vice versa? A market where billions of contracts change hands is impossible if all traders must investigate the creditworthiness of the other trader, or counterparty. The way this credit risk—often called counterparty risk—is managed is a key element of the current reform proposals.

The exchanges deal with the issue of credit risk through a third-party clearinghouse. Once the trade is made on the exchange floor (or electronic network), it goes to the clearinghouse,[5] which guarantees payment to both parties. The process is shown in Figure 1. Traders then do not have to worry about counterparty default: the clearinghouse stands behind all trades. How does the clearinghouse ensure that it can meet its obligations?

Clearing depends on a system of margin, or collateral. Before the trade, both the long and short traders have to deposit an initial margin payment with the clearinghouse to cover potential losses. Then at the end of each trading day, all contracts are repriced, or "marked to market," and all those who have lost money (because prices moved against them) must post additional margin (called variation or maintenance margin) to cover those losses before the next trading session. This is known as a margin call: traders must make good on their losses immediately, or their broker may close out their positions when trading opens the next day. The effect of the margin system is that no one can build up a large paper loss that could damage the clearinghouse in case of default: it is certainly possible to lose large amounts of money trading on the futures exchanges, but only on a "pay as you go" basis.

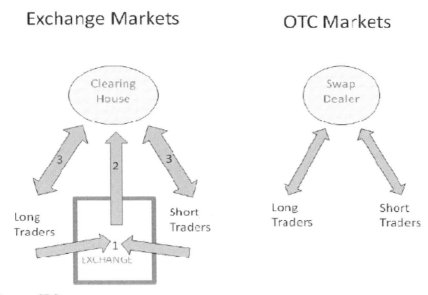

Source: CRS.

Figure 1. Current Derivatives Market Structures: Exchange and Over-the-Counter (OTC).

In the OTC market, as shown in the right side of Figure 1, there is a network of dealers rather than a centralized marketplace. Firms that act as dealers stand ready to take either long or short positions, and make money on spreads and fees. The dealer absorbs the credit risk of customer default, while the customer faces the risk of dealer default. In this kind of market, one would expect the dealers to be the most solid and creditworthy financial institutions, and in fact the OTC market that has emerged is dominated by two or three dozen firms—very large institutions like JP Morgan Chase, Goldman Sachs, Citigroup, and their foreign counterparts. Before 2007, such firms were generally viewed as too well diversified or too well managed to fail; since 2008, they are more likely considered too big to be allowed to fail.

In the OTC market, some contracts require collateral or margin, but not all. There is no standard practice: all contract terms are negotiable. A trade group, the International Swaps and Derivatives Association (ISDA) publishes best practice standards for use of collateral, but compliance is voluntary.

The terms "collateral" and "margin" are similar—both are forms of a downpayment against potential losses to guard against a counterparty's nonpayment—but technically they are not interchangeable. A margining agreement requires that cash or very liquid securities be deposited immediately with the counterparty. After this initial deposit, margin accounts are marked-tomarket, usually daily. In the event of default, the counterparty holding the margin can liquidate the margin account. By contrast, collateral arrangements usually require the counterparty to perfect a lien against the collateral.[6] The range of assets allowable under a collateral agreement is usually wider than what is allowed under margining arrangements.[7] Settlement of collateral shortfalls tends to be less frequent than under margining arrangements.[8]

Because there is no universal, mandatory system of margin, large uncollateralized losses can build up in the OTC market. The best-known example in the crisis was AIG, which wrote about $1.8 trillion worth of credit default swaps guaranteeing payment if certain mortgage-backed securities defaulted or experienced other "credit events."[9] Many of AIG's contracts did require it to post collateral as the credit quality of the underlying securities (or AIG's own credit rating) deteriorated, but AIG did not post initial margin, as this was deemed unnecessary because of the firm's triple-A rating. As the subprime crisis worsened, AIG was subjected to margin calls that it could not meet. To avert bankruptcy, with the risk of global financial chaos, the Federal Reserve and the Treasury put tens of billions of dollars into AIG, the bulk of which went to its derivatives counterparties.[10]

DERIVATIVES REFORM

The AIG case illustrates two aspects of OTC markets that are central to derivatives reform proposals. First, as noted above, AIG was able to amass an OTC derivatives position so large that it threatened to destabilize the entire financial system when the firm suffered unexpected losses, and the risks of default to AIG derivatives counterparties grew. In a market with mandatory clearing and margin, in which AIG would have been required to post initial margin to cover potential losses, there is a stronger possibility that AIG would have run out of money long before the size of its position reached $1.8 trillion.

Second, because OTC contracts are not reported to regulators, the Fed and the Treasury lacked information about which institutions were exposed to AIG, and the size of those exposures. Uncertainty among market participants about the size and distribution of potential derivatives losses flowing from the failure of a major dealer was a factor that exacerbated the "freezing" of credit markets during the peaks of the crisis, and made banks unwilling to lend to each other.

A basic theme in the derivatives reform proposals before the 111th Congress is to get the OTC market to act more like the exchange market—in particular, to have bilateral OTC swaps cleared by a third-party clearing organization. There are some widely recognized benefits to clearing:

- Reduction of counterparty risk—collateral or margin collected by the clearinghouse prevents risk build-ups that could trigger systemic disruptions, and
- Transparency—because information on trades and positions is centralized in the clearinghouse, regulators will know who owes what to whom, improving the ability to respond to a crisis. In addition, as price information becomes public, dealer spreads should narrow, reducing the costs of hedging and other transactions.

At the same time, there are costs associated with a clearing regime that requires all participants to post margin. Firms that use derivatives to hedge business risks take positions that move in the opposite direction to the underlying market. In the example of Southwest Airlines, imagine that energy prices had dropped sharply, instead of rising as they actually did. The reduced fuel costs would have been good for the airline's bottom line, but its derivatives position would have lost money, and had the contracts been cleared, it would have had to post margin to cover those losses. Such losses would not threaten the firm's solvency, because it would still be effectively paying a price for fuel that allowed it to operate at a profit.[11] However, the margin demands could have created liquidity problems. In the current debate, "end users" of OTC derivatives argue that the costs of posting margin may prevent them from hedging, leaving them exposed to greater business risks.

END USERS

The derivatives titles of both the House- and Senate-passed versions of H.R. 4173 include exemptions from clearing requirements intended to avoid placing burdensome costs on end users of derivatives. *End user* is not a term defined in statute or in either version of the bill. In general, it refers to any OTC derivatives counterparty that is not a dealer or a major market participant, although in the current debate it sometimes appears to refer primarily to nonfinancial firms that use derivatives to hedge the risks of their businesses. How much of the OTC market do they account for?

The Bank for International Settlements publishes data on counterparties in several OTC markets. As of December 2009, 33% of OTC contracts were between reporting dealers, 58% were between dealers and other financial institutions, and the remaining 9% involved dealers and nonfinancial entities (see Figure 2).[12]

Thus, nearly two-thirds of OTC derivatives involve an end user. If all end users are exempted from the requirement that OTC swaps be cleared, the market structure problems raised by AIG still remain. That is, if individual dealer firms that retain large amounts of credit risk get into trouble, the government will continue to face an unsatisfactory choice: allow the dealer to fail, and risk panic and cascading failures among interconnected dealers and counterparties, or bail out the dealer using general federal revenues, with the undesirable consequence of reducing incentives for private parties to manage risk prudently.

Derivatives reform legislation seeks to strike a balance. Although the primary goal is to eliminate the problem of derivatives dealers that are too big or too interconnected to fail, the House and Senate bill versions provide exemptions for end users whose derivatives positions are intended to hedge business risk and who are not thought to pose systemic risk. The bill versions differ in the way they define classes of market participants who are to be subject to the mandatory clearing requirement (as well as other forms of regulation) and in the way the exemptions are structured.

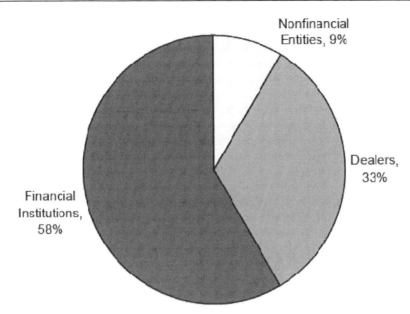

Source: CRS, using data from Bank for International Settlements.
Notes: Includes OTC interest rate, foreign currency, credit default swaps and equity-linked derivative contracts.

Figure 2. OTC Swap Counterparties, December 2009.

LEGISLATIVE PROPOSALS AND EXEMPTIONS FOR END USERS

The Derivative Markets Transparency and Accountability Act was passed by the House as Title III of its version of the comprehensive financial reform bill, H.R. 4173. On May 20, 2010, the Senate passed its version of H.R. 4173. Title VII of the Senate bill deals with the regulation of OTC derivatives. Both the House and Senate versions are based on the Obama Administration's proposed legislative language as a base text, but depart from the model in significant ways.

Table 1 below sets out a comparison of the derivatives provisions and exemptions in H.R. 4173, as passed by the House, and as passed by the Senate, respectively.

Table 1. Comparison of Derivatives Titles of H.R. 4173, as Passed by the House and Senate, respectively

Provision	House Version (Derivatives Title)	Senate Version (Derivatives Title)
Who wields regulatory authority?	After consulting with the Securities and Exchange Commission (SEC) and prudential regulators such as the Federal Reserve, Office of the Comptroller of the Currency (OCC), and Federal Deposit Insurance Corporation (FDIC), the Commodities Futures Trading Commission (CFTC) has rule-making authority over swaps. SEC has rule-making authority over security-based swaps after consulting with CFTC and Prudential Regulators. The CFTC and the SEC are not required to undertake joint rule-making on most issues. If, however, one of the agencies feels that the other one is encroaching upon its territory, that agency can file a petition for review of the rule by the D.C. Circuit U.S. Court of Appeals. The Treasury, CFTC and SEC shall conduct a joint study of the desirability and feasibility of establishing, by January 1, 2012, a single regulator for financial derivatives. (§3005)	Most rule-making is either by CFTC alone or by the SEC alone. CFTC alone has rule-making authority over swaps. For instance, the CFTC alone issues rules to determine which swaps or category of swaps must be cleared. The CFTC issues rules further defining who is a major swap participant, and who is an end-user. For security-based swaps, the SEC will issue rules further defining who is considered a major security-based swap participant (MSBSP), based on the definition given in §761. The SEC alone also issues rules defining which type of security-based swaps must be cleared. The SEC also issues rules determining what constitutes a "substantial threshold" for security-based swaps, to be considered a MSBSP. (§761)

Provision	House Version (Derivatives Title)	Senate Version (Derivatives Title)
How is swap defined?	Amends the Commodity Exchange Act (CEA) to include a very broad definition of swaps.	Similar broad definition of swaps. Swaps based on any broad-based index, including broad-based securities indices, are considered "swaps," and given to the CFTC to regulate. "Security-based swaps" fall to the SEC.
	Foreign exchange swaps and forward contracts are excluded. However, if the CFTC determines that either foreign exchange swaps or foreign exchange forwards should be regulated as swaps and the Treasury concurs, then they shall be regulated as swaps. In this case, CFTC and Treasury will then jointly determine which powers the CFTC will exercise over foreign exchange swaps and foreign exchange forwards, and those powers will be exercised solely by the CFTC. (§3101(35)(D)(i))	Only swaps based on narrow indices, single securities or loans, and single-reference entity swaps (such as credit default swaps based on a single entity or narrow index) are considered security-based swaps. (§761)
		The bill includes foreign exchange swaps and foreign exchange forwards as swaps, which would bring them under CFTC regulation, unless the Treasury makes a written determination that they should not be regulated as swaps. In that case, they must still be reported to swap repositories, or to the CFTC if no such repository will accept them. This is similar to the treatment in the House version of H.R. 4173. (§721)
	Any transaction with the U.S. government or a federal government agency expressly backed by the full faith and credit of the U.S. government as a counterparty is excluded. Identified banking products, under the Legal Certainty for Bank Products Act of 2000, are excluded from the definition of "security-based swap," from CFTC regulation, and from coverage by the Commodity Exchange Act. There may, however, be exceptions to these exclusions for identified banking products. (§3103)	Amends The Legal Certainty for Bank Products Act of 2000 to state that the CFTC will have no authority over identified banking products. Also states that the definition of "security-based swap" in section 3(a)(68) of the Securities Exchange Act of 1934 does not include any identified bank product. Then provides for certain exceptions at regulators' discretion. (§725)

Table 1. (Continued)

Provision	House Version (Derivatives Title)	Senate Version (Derivatives Title)
Who is a "major swap participant"?	A major swap participant is anyone who is not a swap dealer that: maintains a substantial net position in outstanding swaps, excluding positions held primarily for hedging, reducing or otherwise mitigating its commercial risk, including operating and balance sheet risk; or whose outstanding swaps create substantial net counterparty exposure among the aggregate of its counterparties that could expose those counterparties to significant credit losses. (§ 3201) BUT NOTE: § 3307 of this same Act later differently defines a major swap participant as anyone who is not a swap dealer that: maintains a substantial net position in outstanding swaps, excluding positions held primarily for hedging, reducing or otherwise mitigating its commercial risk; or whose outstanding swaps create substantial net counterparty exposure that could have serious adverse effects on the financial stability of the U.S. banking system or financial markets. (§3307) NOTE: The CFTC will define by rule or regulation the following terms: substantial net position, substantial net counterparty exposure, and significant credit losses.	Anyone who is not a swap dealer and who EITHER: (I) maintains a substantial position in swaps for any of the major swap categories as determined by the CFTC, excluding: (a) positions held for hedging or mitigating commercial risk; and (b) positions maintained by any employee benefit plan (or any contract held by such a plan) as defined in paragraphs (3) and (32) of §3 of the Employee Retirement Income Security Act of 1974, for the primary purpose of hedging or mitigating any risk directly associated with the operation of the plan; OR (II) whose outstanding swaps create substantial counterparty exposure that could have serious adverse effects on the financial stability of the U.S. banking system or financial markets; OR (III) (i) is a financial entity, other than an entity predominantly engaged in providing financing for the purchase of an affiliate's merchandise or manufactured goods, that is highly leveraged relative to the amount of capital it holds; AND (III) (ii) maintains a substantial position in outstanding swaps in any major swap category as determined by the CFTC. (§ 721)

Provision	House Version (Derivatives Title)	Senate Version (Derivatives Title)
Who is a "major security-based swap participant"?	A major security-based swap participant is anyone who is not a swap dealer that: maintains a substantial net position in outstanding security-based swaps, excluding positions held primarily for hedging, reducing or otherwise mitigating its commercial risk, including operating and balance sheet risk; or whose outstanding security-based swaps create substantial net counterparty exposure among the aggregate of its counterparties that could expose those counterparties to significant credit losses. (§3201) BUT NOTE: § 3307 of this same Act later differently defines a major security-based swap participant as anyone who is not a swap dealer that: maintains a substantial net position in outstanding swaps, excluding positions held primarily for hedging, reducing or otherwise mitigating its commercial risk; or whose outstanding swaps create substantial net counterparty exposure that could have serious adverse effects on the financial stability of the U.S. banking system or financial markets.	The CFTC will define the term "substantial position" at the threshold it determines to be prudent for the effective monitoring, management, and oversight of entities that are systemically important or can significantly impact the financial system of the U.S. (§721) Any person who is not a security-based swap dealer and who EITHER: (I) maintains a substantial position in security-based swaps for any of the major security-based swaps categories determined by the SEC, excluding: (a) positions held for hedging or mitigating commercial risk; and (b) positions maintained by any employee benefit plan (or any contract held by such a plan) as defined in paragraphs (3) and (32) of §3 of the Employee Retirement Income Security Act of 1974, for the primary purpose of hedging or mitigating any risk directly associated with the operation of the plan; OR (II) whose outstanding security-based swaps create substantial counterparty exposure that could have serious adverse effects on the financial stability of the U.S. banking system or financial markets; OR (III) (i) is a financial entity that is highly leveraged relative to the amount of capital it holds;

Table 1. (Continued)

Provision	House Version (Derivatives Title)	Senate Version (Derivatives Title)
	(§3307) The SEC will define by rule or regulation "a substantial net position."	AND (III) (ii) maintains a substantial position in outstanding security-based swaps in any major security-based swap category as determined by the SEC. (§761) The SEC will define the term "substantial position" at the threshold it determines to be prudent for the effective monitoring, management, and oversight of entities that are systemically important or can significantly impact the financial system of the U.S. (§761)
Which derivatives must be cleared?	A swap must be cleared if a registered derivatives clearing organization (DCO) will accept the swap for clearing, and if the CFTC has determined that the type of swap should be required to be cleared. The CFTC will initiate its own review of all categories of swaps and determine which categories should be required to be cleared regardless of whether a DCO has applied to clear them. (§3103 (j))	The CFTC shall issue rules as to which categories or types of swaps must be cleared. A swap must be cleared if it meets the criteria set forth by the CFTC, and if a registered derivatives clearing organization (DCO) accepts the swap for clearing. EXCEPTION: There is a broad, automatic exception to the clearing requirement called the "End User Clearing Exemption." (§ 723) "Commercial end users" are entitled to this end user clearing exemption.

Provision	House Version (Derivatives Title)	Senate Version (Derivatives Title)
	EXCEPTION: There is a fairly broad, automatic exception to the clearing requirement for so-called "end users"—which means a counterparty who is not a swap dealer or a major swap participant (MSP). This says that the clearing requirement shall not apply to a swap if one of the counterparties to the swap is not a swap dealer or major swap participant; and is using swaps to hedge or mitigate commercial risk, including operating or balance sheet risk; and notifies the CFTC how it generally meets its financial obligations associated with entering into non-cleared swaps. (§3103)	A "commercial end user" is defined as any person, other than a financial entity, who, as its primary business activity, owns, uses, produces, processes, manufactures, distributes, merchandises, or markets goods, services or commodities (which shall include but not be limited to coal, natural gas, electricity, ethanol, crude oil, gasoline, propane, distillates, and other hydrocarbons) either individually or in a fiduciary capacity. (§723) If one counterparty to the swap is such an end user, then that counterparty can elect not to clear the swap, so long as that end user "is using the swap to hedge its own commercial risk." A "financial entity" (not entitled to the end user exemption) is defined as anyone who is EITHER: (i) a swap dealer, MSP, security-based swap dealer, or security-based MSP; OR (ii) a person predominantly engaged in activities that are in the business of banking or financial in nature, as defined in Section 4(k) of the Bank

Table 1. (Continued)

Provision	House Version (Derivatives Title)	Senate Version (Derivatives Title)
		Holding Company Act of 1956; OR (iii) a person predominantly engaged in activities that are financial in nature; OR (iv) a commodity pool or private fund as defined in §202(a) of the Investment Advisers Act; OR (v) a person required to register with the CFTC. An affiliate of an end user (including affiliates predominantly engaged in providing financing for the merchandise or manufactured goods of the commercial end user) may only elect not to clear its swaps if the affiliate uses the swap to hedge or mitigate the commercial risk of the commercial end user parent company, or other affiliates of the commercial end user, who are not financial entities. An affiliate cannot use this exemption if the affiliate is a swap dealer, MSP, security-based swap dealer, major security-based swap participant, bank holding company with over $50 billion in assets, commodity pool, or certain investment companies.

Provision	House Version (Derivatives Title)	Senate Version (Derivatives Title)
		(§723) The definition of end user could arguably include a broad range of derivatives users. Any company that uses commodities to produce goods as part of its primary business – such as most manufacturers – and any company that markets services as part of its primary business – excepting financial services—would appear to be included, and would thus be exempt from having to clear their swaps through clearinghouses.

The end user exemption for security-based swaps is identical to that for swaps, with the same conditions for affiliates of end users. (§763) |
| Any provisions to potentially restrict or prohibit swaps trading by banks? | Nothing similar to the Senate's section 716 proposal exists in the House version of H.R. 4173. | Section 716 says that "notwithstanding any other provision of law (including regulations), no federal assistance may be provided to any swaps entity with respect to any swap, security-based swap, or other activity of the swaps entity."

It defines "federal assistance" to mean the use of any funds, including advances from any Federal Reserve credit facility or discount window, FDIC insurance, or guarantees for the purpose of:
(a) making any loan to, or purchasing any stock, equity interest, or debt obligation of, any swap entity;
(b) purchasing the assets of any swaps entity;
(c) guaranteeing any loan or debt issuance of any swaps entity; or |

Table 1. (Continued)

Provision	House Version (Derivatives Title)	Senate Version (Derivatives Title)
		(d) entering into any assistance arrangement (including tax breaks), loss sharing or profit sharing with any swaps entity. It defines "swaps entity" as any swap dealer or security-based swap dealer, MSP or security-based MSP, exchange, swap execution facility, DCO, central counterparty (for clearing) or clearinghouse. (§716) Another title of the Senate's version of H.R. 4173, Title VI, includes §619, often dubbed "the Volcker rule," which includes a prohibition on proprietary trading by an insured depository institution, a company that controls one, or a bank holding company. "Proprietary trading" is defined as purchasing or selling, or otherwise acquiring or disposing of, stocks, bonds, options, commodities, derivatives, or other financial instruments, for the trading book of the institution itself, or for such other portfolio as the federal banking agencies may determine. But it does not include purchasing or selling these instruments on behalf of a customer, as part of market making activities, or otherwise in connection with or in facilitation of customer relationships, including risk-mitigating hedging activities related to the purchase or sale of those instruments. Federal banking regulators are to issue further guidance. (§619)

Provision	House Version (Derivatives Title)	Senate Version (Derivatives Title)
		This section apparently also seeks to restrict derivatives activities of FDIC-insured banks, and companies that control them. However, it distinguishes between market-making, risk-mitigating hedging, and transactions on behalf of a customer – which are permitted - versus "proprietary trading" for the bank's own book – which is not permitted.
What exchange-trading requirements are there?	A swap that is required to be cleared must be traded either on a designated contract market (for example, a regulated futures exchange), or through a swap execution facility registered with the CFTC. EXCEPTION: This requirement does not apply if no designated contract market or swap execution facility makes the swap available for trading. In this case, the swap will still be subject to reporting and record-keeping requirements. Core principles for a swap execution facility are set out in the act. These include monitoring trading activities, adopting position limits, providing information to the CFTC upon request, keeping business records for five years, making data public on trading volume, prices, and other information as required by the CFTC. (§3109)	Swaps subject to the clearing requirement must be traded on a designated contract market (DCM) or registered swap execution facility, unless no DCM or swap execution facility will accept the swap for trading. If a commercial end user is subject to the clearing exemption, they can also elect to be automatically exempted from this exchange-trading requirement. Also, if no DCO will accept the swap for clearing, then the CFTC shall exempt the swap from the exchange-trading requirement as well. (§723). Amends the Commodity Exchange Act to require that no-one may operate a facility for trading or processing swaps unless it is registered as a swap execution facility or as a designated contract market (§733).

Table 1. (Continued)

Provision	House Version (Derivatives Title)	Senate Version (Derivatives Title)
		The facility must register with the CFTC even if already registered with the SEC. A security-based swap subject to the clearing requirement shall not be traded except on a national securities exchange, or on a registered security-based swap execution facility. Such facilities must register with the SEC even if they are already registered with the CFTC. If no national securities exchange or security-based swap execution facility makes the security-based swap available for trading, then that swap will be subject to reporting and record-keeping requirements to be determined by the SEC. (§763)
What capital and margin requirements are there?	Each registered swap dealer which is a regulated bank, and each major swap participant for which there is a prudential regulator shall meet such minimum capital requirements and minimum initial and variation margin requirements (for uncleared swaps) as the prudential regulators shall prescribe by rule or regulation. Non-bank swap dealers and major swap participants without a prudential regulator shall meet such minimum capital requirements and minimum initial and variation margin requirements as the CFTC shall prescribe.	Capital and margin requirements appear to apply to MSPs and swap dealers (and security-based MSPs and swap dealers) only. Capital requirements will be set higher for bank and non-bank swap dealers and major swap participants for swaps that are not cleared. Each registered swap dealer and MSP that is a depository institution as defined in §3 of the Federal Deposit Insurance Act shall meet such minimum capital requirements and minimum initial and variation margin requirements as the appropriate federal banking agency, in consultation with the CFTC and SEC, shall prescribe by rule or regulation to help ensure the safety and soundness of the swap dealer or MSP.

Provision	House Version (Derivatives Title)	Senate Version (Derivatives Title)
	There are no provisions authorizing the CFTC, SEC or banking regulators to impose capital or margin requirements for uncleared swaps on "end users" who are neither swap dealers, security-based swap dealers, major swap participants nor security-based swap participants.	(§731) Non-bank swap dealers and MSPs shall meet such minimum capital requirements and minimum initial and variation margin requirements as the CFTC and SEC shall prescribe by rule or regulation based on the same two factors above. Margin (initial and variation) will be imposed by regulators only on uncleared swaps. (§731). Initial and variation margin requirements must be at least as strict for non-bank swap dealers and MSPs as for bank dealers and MSPs. (§731) The CFTC, for non-banks, and the banking regulators, for banks, may permit the use of non-cash collateral. (§731) A similar provision applies for security-based swaps (§764). EXCEPTION: For transactions in which one counterparty is not a swap dealer, MSP, or financial entity, the minimum initial and variation margin requirements will not apply. (§731) There is thus an automatic exemption from margin requirements for uncleared swaps for those who are neither swap dealers, MSPs, nor financial entities. The same exemption is included for security-based swaps. (§764) For security-based swaps, capital and margin requirements are the same, except that the SEC will prescribe rules for non-bank security-based MSPs and dealers; and the banking regulators will prescribe them for security-based MSPs and swap dealers who are banks. (§764)

Table 1. (Continued)

Provision	House Version (Derivatives Title)	Senate Version (Derivatives Title)
What reporting requirements are there?	All swaps that are not accepted for clearing by any derivatives clearing organization shall be reported either to a swap repository, or, if there is no repository that would accept the swap, to the CFTC. Swaps entered into before enactment of this act shall be reported within 6 months to a swap repository or to the CFTC. Swaps entered into after enactment of this act shall be reported within three months, or other time period the CFTC may prescribe by rule.	All swaps not accepted for clearing by a DCO must be reported to a repository, or if no repository accepts the swap for reporting, to the CFTC. Both counterparties to a swap that is not cleared by a DCO shall report the swap. (§723) BUT NOTE: §729 then states under "Reporting Obligations" that uncleared swaps must be reported as above, but if only one counterparty is a swap dealer or MSP, then only that counterparty will report the swap. If one is a swap dealer and the other an MSP, then the dealer will report. In all other cases, the counterparties may select which one will report the swap. (§729) All security-based swaps not accepted for clearing by a DCO must be reported to a repository, or if no repository accepts the swap for reporting, to the SEC. If only one counterparty is a security-based swap dealer or MSP, then only that counterparty will report the swap. If one is a security-based swap dealer and the other a security-based MSP, then the dealer will report. In all other cases, the counterparties may select which one will report the swap. (§766)

Source: Analysis by CRS.

Key Issues in Derivatives Reform

Some basic elements are present in both the House and Senate versions of the bill. First, transactions between swap dealers and major swap participants (MSPs) must be cleared, as long as a derivatives clearing organization will accept the swap and the appropriate regulators approve the swap for clearing. The purpose of this exception is twofold: (1) clearinghouses should not be forced to clear contracts that might pose risks to their solvency (as might be the case if a contract were highly customized, complex, difficult to price, or if the risk exposure of a class of contracts were concentrated in a single dealer), and (2) the regulatory approval requirement ensures that there will not be a "race to the bottom" among clearinghouses, in which competition for market share and clearing fees leads to imprudent risk taking.

Although generally similar, the House and Senate versions differ in some crucial elements, particularly in the exemption from the mandatory clearing requirement, which has featured prominently in the political debate. Other differences include the Senate version's Section 716 prohibiting federal assistance to any swaps entity, which the House version lacks, and which has also generated controversy. This provision has been described in the press as forcing banks to spin off their derivatives trading.

In terms of exemptions from the clearing requirement, "end-users" of derivatives—financial and nonfinancial firms that use the contracts to reduce, or hedge, business risks—argue that the cost of hedging will become excessive if they are forced to post margin or collateral to a clearinghouse. The scope of the exemptions for end-users is determined in two ways:

- **Which types of derivatives must be cleared?** Both bill versions require clearing only of swaps that are accepted by a derivatives clearing organization (DCO) and are approved for clearing by regulators. DCOs are presumably less likely to accept for clearing derivatives that are highly customized and complex, or illiquidly traded, as this makes it harder for the DCO to properly evaluate the risks inherent in the derivative. This tends to make it harder for the DCO to accurately estimate margin requirements and increases risk to the DCO.
- **Who must clear their derivatives?** The House version automatically exempts swaps from clearing where one counterparty is (1) neither a swap dealer nor a major swap participant; (2) using swaps to hedge commercial risk; and (3) notifies regulators how it normally meets its financial obligations in connection to uncleared swaps. In the House version, the definition of a "major swap participant" is crucial because

it determines the scope of exemptions from the clearing requirement. In the Senate version, however, a swap is automatically exempt from clearing if one counterparty qualifies as a "commercial end user." A "commercial end user" is broadly defined to encompass almost any company whose primary business activity is non-financial.

As noted, the question of who is a "major swap participant" (MSP) in the House version is important, as it determines the scope of exemptions from clearing. The House version actually contains two different definitions of an MSP—first in Section 3101, the "Definitions" section, and then later, in Section 3307.[13] Based on the first definition, an MSP is one who maintains a substantial net position in outstanding swaps (excluding positions held primarily for hedging or mitigating commercial risk, including operating and balance sheet risk), or whose outstanding swaps create substantial net counterparty exposure among the aggregate of its counterparties that could expose those counterparties to significant credit losses.[14] The House version directs regulators to define the "substantial" and "significant" thresholds at levels appropriate to entities that are systemically important or can significantly impact the financial system through counterparty credit risk. Under this definition of an MSP, regulators would presumably define the threshold amount at a fairly high level, to be systemically significant. Also, the exclusion of swaps held to mitigate commercial, operating or balance sheet risk would presumably exclude many swaps, as well.

In determining who is an MSP, the Senate version similarly instructs the CFTC to define the term "substantial position" at a threshold it determines to be prudent for the effective monitoring, management, and oversight of entities that are systemically important or can significantly impact the financial system of the U.S. a whole. Yet, in the Senate version, it is the definition of "commercial end user," not MSP, that determines the scope of the automatic clearing exemption. Whether or not an entity is an MSP determines instead whether it must register with the CFTC or the SEC, and whether it will be subject to capital and margin requirements for uncleared swaps, to be set by regulators, as discussed in the next section.

Because both versions of the bill allow regulators substantial discretion in writing rules and defining terms, it is difficult to say with precision how much of the currently unregulated OTC derivatives market would be moved onto centralized clearinghouses under either bill. It appears, however, that regulators' discretion in the House version to determine who is an MSP, and thus who must clear their derivatives, may be broader in scope and could result in a greater share of swaps continuing to trade OTC than would be the case under the Senate version.

This is largely because the Senate version restricts its automatic clearing exemption to nonfinancial firms, whereas the House version does not. As Figure 2 above demonstrated, the Bank for International Settlements estimated that only about 10% of OTC derivatives involved a nonfinancial entity. Given the restriction on "commercial end users" as primarily non-financial in the Senate version, regulators appear to have less leeway to exempt derivatives from clearing for the bulk of OTC trades under the Senate bill. In addition, under the House version, in determining who is an MSP and thus who must clear their derivatives, regulators must establish a threshold for what constitutes having a "substantial net position" of outstanding swaps, for the purpose of the clearing requirement, at a level that would threaten overall financial stability.

SAFEGUARDS APPLICABLE TO UNCLEARED OTC SWAPS

If end-user exemptions are too broad, some portion of the systemic risks posed by the unregulated OTC markets will remain. In recognition of this, the House and Senate versions of the bill to differing degrees provide additional safeguards against the impact of defaults by traders (or dealers) in uncleared swaps. One such safeguard is that, in addition to the clearing requirement, dealers and MSPs will be subject to prudential capital requirements under the House and Senate proposals, to cushion them against the impact of derivatives losses. Under both proposals, swap dealers and MSPs that are banks will have capital requirements and margin requirements, for swaps that a clearinghouse will not clear, set by their primary banking regulator. Non-bank swap dealers and MSPs will have capital and margin requirements set by the CFTC and SEC.

Another safeguard, as mentioned, has to do with the imposition of margin requirements on uncleared contracts. Both bill versions direct the regulators to impose initial and variation margin requirements on contracts that are not cleared through a derivatives clearing organization. In both versions, regulators are given authority to impose capital and margin requirements only on swaps where both parties to the swap are either an MSP or a swap dealer.

HYPOTHETICAL EXAMPLES

To give some hypothetical examples, a small nonfinancial hedger whose counterparty was a dealer like Goldman Sachs would probably not have to clear its swaps under either the House or Senate versions of H.R. 4173. Under the House version, in the event that the firm defaulted, the effect on the dealer would probably not be material or significant. Under the Senate version, because the firm was primarily nonfinancial in nature, it would automatically be exempted from the clearing requirement as a "commercial end user."

In the case of a large industrial company, like Coca-Cola, it is more difficult to judge the effect under the House version, because regulatory discretion would be involved in administering the provisions of the statute. A company like Coca-Cola is likely to have very large derivatives positions to hedge foreign exchange, interest rate, and commodity price risk, and risks incurred by the financial assets on its balance sheet. By size alone, its positions could meet the "substantial net position" test of the House version, as determined by a regulator. But it might also characterize its position as hedging commercial risk, and so be excluded from the MSP definition. It is less likely that its outstanding net position in swaps would pose a risk to the financial system as a whole, however—as per the House proposal's minimum-threshold standard that the regulator must follow in setting the level of swaps that constitute a substantial net position. Under the Senate's version, since Coca-Cola is primarily nonfinancial in nature, it should presumably meet the definition of a commercial end user, and thus be automatically exempt from clearing.

Assuming that Coca-Cola's outstanding net position in swaps did meet the minimum threshold for an MSP under the House version, a question would then be whether a hypothetical default by Coca-Cola on its derivatives obligations would cause significant or material harm to its counterparties—under the first definition given in the House version of H.R. 4173[15]. Under the second definition,[16] the question would be whether a hypothetical default by Coca-Cola on its derivatives obligations would cause such harm to the financial system as a whole. In both cases, regulators would need to exercise judgment on a number of factors: was the position concentrated with a single dealer, or dispersed among a number of firms? What, under current market conditions, was the capacity of the dealer or dealers to absorb a loss of a given size? Was the financial system able to withstand the shock at that particular time?

SECTION 716

As mentioned, the House and Senate versions of H.R. 4173 also differ in that the Senate version includes a provision in its Section 716 that would prohibit federal assistance to any swaps entity with respect to any swap, security-based swap, or other activity of the swaps entity. Federal assistance is defined to include access to the Federal Reserve's discount window or advances from any Federal Reserve credit facility, FDIC insurance, and other types of assistance or guarantees enumerated in the bill, which, taken together, are crucial for depository institutions. No similar provision exists in the House version. Section 716 has provoked controversy. Some are concerned that it could in practice end up increasing systemic risk and weaken oversight of the financial system.[17]

End Notes

[1] For a description of the mechanics of these contracts, see CRS Report R40646, *Derivatives Regulation in the 111th Congress*, by Mark Jickling and Rena S. Miller.

[2] See Bank for International Settlements (BIS), Table 23B, for year 2000 turnover for derivative financial instruments traded on organized exchanges, available at http://www.bis.org/publ/qtrpdf/r_qa0206.pdf. For December 2008 figures for derivatives traded on organized exchanges, see BIS Quarterly Review, September 2009, International Banking and Financial Market Developments, available at http://www.bis.org/publ/qtrpdf/r_qt0909.pdf.

[3] See Bank for International Settlements (BIS), Statistical Annex, Table 19, December, 2000 figure for notional amount of total OTC contracts, available at http://www.bis.org/publ/qtrpdf/r_qa0206.pdf. See Bank for International Settlements (BIS), BIS Quarterly Review, September 2009, Statistical Annex, Table 19, for December 2008 figure for notional amount of total OTC contracts, available at http://www.bis.org/publ/qtrpdf/r_qa0909.pdf.

[4] Federal Reserve, *Flow of Funds Accounts of the United States*, September 17, 2009, accessible at http://www.federalreserve.gov/releases/z1/Current/z1r-1.pdf.

[5] Also referred to as a central counterparty or as (in the statutory phrase) a derivatives clearing organization (DCO).

[6] To perfect a lien means following certain procedures required by law in order to create a security interest that is enforceable.

[7] Office of the Comptroller of the Currency, *Risk Management of Financial Derivatives*, January, 1997, Appendix J, "Credit Enhancements," p. 183, accessible at http://www.occ.treas.gov/handbook/deriv.pdf.

[8] Ibid.

[9] The credit events that trigger credit swap payments may include ratings downgrades, debt restructuring, late payment of interest or principal, as well as default.

[10] For an account of this process, see Office of the Special Inspector General for the Troubled Asset Relief Program ("SIGTARP"), *Factors Affecting Efforts to Limit Payments to AIG Counterparties*, November 17, 2009.

[11] In other words, a hedging strategy locks in the price that prevails at the time the contract is made. If the firm loses money at that price, it will not hedge.

[12] The markets covered are interest rate, foreign exchange, credit default swaps and equity derivatives. The total notional value of these contracts was $538.2 trillion. Bank for International Settlements, *Semiannual OTC derivatives statistics at December 2009*, accessible at http://www.bis.org/statistics/derdetailed.htm.

[13] For the exact definitions, please see Table 1 above.

[14] Section 3101 of the House version of H.R. 4173.

[15] Section 3101 of the House version of H.R. 4173.

[16] Section 3307 of the House version of H.R. 4173.

[17] See for example, the letter from Federal Reserve Chairman Ben Bernanke posted by The Wall Street Journal at http://blogs

In: Derivatives Reform and Regulation
Editor: Aidan B. Lynch

ISBN: 978-1-61324-935-2
© 2011 Nova Science Publishers, Inc.

Chapter 2

DERIVATIVES REGULATION IN THE 111TH CONGRESS[*]

Mark Jickling and Rena S. Miller

SUMMARY

In the wake of the financial crisis and unusual oil price volatility, new attention was drawn to the regulation of derivatives—and particularly toward the unregulated over-the-counter (OTC) derivatives market. What regulatory changes, if any, would reduce risks to the financial system from derivatives trading? A number of bills were introduced in the 111th Congress, and several congressional committees have held hearings. The Dodd-Frank Wall Street Reform and Consumer Protection Act (P.L. 111-203) enacted a sweeping reform of derivatives trading and oversight and brought the unregulated OTC swaps market under the jurisdiction of federal regulators.

The 111th Congress proposals for reform ran the gamut from requiring all derivatives trading to occur on regulated exchanges— essentially shutting down the unregulated OTC market that exists today— to permitting OTC trading to continue, but with more disclosure and oversight. Some participants in the OTC markets have noted that the lack of transparency is in and of itself an attraction, allowing them to take large speculative positions without other market participants being aware of their identities or trading positions. In the crisis, however, this lack of

---

[*] This is an edited, reformatted and augmented version of a Congressional Research Service publication, CRS Report for Congress R40646, from www.crs.gov, dated March 3, 2011.

transparency appears to have exacerbated fears about potential losses faced by financial institutions and made banks less willing to lend. Dodd-Frank requires that all OTC derivatives be reported to swap data repositories, and that key market information be made public.

Before Dodd-Frank, various derivative products were subject to different legal frameworks. The Commodity Futures Trading Commission (CFTC) was the lead federal agency, but the Securities and Exchange Commission (SEC), the Federal Reserve, and other banking regulators also had jurisdictional claims. Under Dodd-Frank, this regulatory complexity continues, with the SEC given jurisdiction over most security-based swaps, the CFTC regulating other swaps, and the other regulators in a variety of consulting roles.

A key OTC market reform is to mandate the use of central counterparties (CCPs)—or clearinghouses—to process derivatives trades and thereby hopefully reduce risk and increase transparency. (Such clearinghouses have long been a standard feature of the regulated futures exchanges.) The Dodd-Frank Act included an exemption from the clearing requirement for nonfinancial end-users, who use derivatives to hedge the commercial risks of their businesses.

Additional proposals focused on new record-keeping or reporting requirements for OTC trades; audit trails; position limits; large trader reporting requirements; and increasing regulatory oversight of trading. An additional important question, for which Congress's tools may be limited, is how to ensure regulatory harmonization with other international markets, so as to avoid a "race to the bottom" in derivatives regulation.

This report summarizes other derivatives legislation that was considered but not enacted by the 111th Congress, and it provides background on the derivatives market.

INTRODUCTION

Derivative financial instruments have been among the fastest-growing segments of financial markets in recent decades. Proponents argued that derivatives would enhance risk management and make price discovery mechanisms more transparent. Since 2007, however, price volatility in energy and other commodities has been extraordinary, and the global financial system has become unstable. As a result, new attention has been drawn to the regulation of derivatives markets—and particularly toward the unregulated over-the-counter (OTC) derivatives market, where transactions are not made on a public exchange market and where little information on trading and prices is available. Do regulators need more information or supervisory authority over OTC derivatives? Is their existing authority sufficient to prevent excessive speculation and price volatility in the markets they do regulate? What regulatory changes, if any, would reduce risks to the financial system from derivatives trading? In the spring of 2009, the Obama Administration proposed legislative changes to overhaul regulation of OTC derivatives. A number of bills have been introduced in the 111th Congress, and several congressional committees have held hearings.

DERIVATIVE FINANCE

Derivatives are financial instruments or contracts whose value rises or falls with fluctuations in the price of an underlying commodity or financial variable. There are several forms of derivatives—the best-known are futures contracts, options, and swap agreements[1]—but all have this common central feature: two parties promise to make a transaction (or series of transactions) in the future at a price that is agreed upon today. It is expected that the underlying price or rate will fluctuate over the life of the contract, but the price specified in the derivative instrument remains fixed. If they succeed in forecasting the direction of prices, derivatives traders will be entitled to buy the underlying commodity for less (or sell for more) than the going market price. For every winner, there is a loser. Thus, futures markets are "zero-sum"—any change in the price of the underlying commodity generates profits for some traders, and an equal amount of losses for the rest.

Derivatives are sometimes described as bets on the direction of future price trends. As prices rise and fall, derivatives traders make profits or losses, even though they may never own the underlying commodity itself.[2] Questions then arise: what separates derivatives from gambling? What public interest is served by the activity? There are two recognized benefits to derivatives trading: *hedging* and *price discovery*.

Hedgers are traders who use the market to avoid price risk arising from their commercial dealings in the underlying commodity. A cattle producer, for example, can use the markets to lock in today's price for future sales of livestock, obtaining protection against the risk of falling prices. The producer may purchase futures contracts that gain value if the price of live cattle falls.[3] If the price does in fact drop by the time the futures position expires, the producer will earn less money on physical sales, but the loss will be offset by futures contract profits. Conversely, if prices rise, the producer will lose money on the futures contracts, but gain on physical sales. Whichever way prices move, the net result is the same: the risk of unfavorable price movements over the term of the futures contracts has been eliminated, or hedged.

Credit default swaps—another type of derivative contract—can also be used to hedge risk, even if the trader does not own the underlying bond. For example, a company that supplies auto parts to General Motors and depends on payments from GM might purchase a credit default swap on a GM bond to hedge against the risk of a GM default. The auto parts company would make a stream of payments to the seller of the credit default swap, and in case of a GM default, bankruptcy or other credit event, the CDS seller would pay the parts company a lump sum. If GM defaulted, the loss of payments to the auto parts company would be partly offset by the lump-sum payment the parts supplier would receive from its credit default swap counterparty. The ability to manage various forms of risk with futures, swaps, and other derivatives enables firms to budget, invest, and produce more efficiently, and provides a buffer against adverse price shocks.

Who takes on the price risk that the hedger gets rid of? It will probably be a speculator who never actually handles the physical commodity, but simply seeks to profit by forecasting future prices. Most trading in derivatives is speculative;[4] the futures exchanges are associations of professional speculators. The advantage of a large volume of trading is that hedgers can quickly find someone to take the opposite side of their trade. For instance, a firm that is at risk if energy prices rise (such as an airline or a power utility) can instantly find a counterparty who is willing to bet that prices will fall, enabling the hedging firm to lock in the current price.

Price discovery is the second benefit. Centralized marketplaces like the futures exchanges are forums where all available information about supply and demand for the underlying commodity is assembled and incorporated into the price. Traders' decisions to buy or sell are guided by data on current inventories and consumption, expectations about long-term supply and demand trends, macroeconomic conditions, geopolitical risk factors that could disrupt supply, assessments of market psychology, and innumerable other considerations. A central tenet of free market economics is that a competitive market, where no participant is able to manipulate or dictate prices, is the best available mechanism for determining prices that will ensure that supply meets demand and that resources are efficiently allocated. The price generated by the futures exchanges is publicly available: industrial firms, financial institutions, small businesses, and consumers may all use it to allocate their resources efficiently.

However, when commodity prices show extreme volatility, as in the case of crude oil since 2007, theoretical justifications of free market dynamics are not satisfactory. At such times, policymakers may wish to examine the internal workings of the derivatives markets much more closely than under normal conditions.

Types of Derivatives Markets (Pre-Dodd-Frank)

Derivatives markets can be divided into two classes: regulated exchange markets, where standardized contracts are traded in great volume, and the OTC market, where contracts can be (but are not always) highly customized and where deals can be made in private between two counterparties. In the United States, major derivatives exchanges are regulated by the Commodity Futures Trading Commission (CFTC, which oversees the futures exchanges) and by the Securities and Exchange Commission (SEC, which regulates stock option markets). SEC and CFTC regulation of exchanges is generally similar: federal law requires both securities and commodity exchanges to make and enforce rules to ensure fair and orderly trading and to protect public investors from fraud. Many classes of market professionals, as well as the exchanges themselves, are required to register with a federal agency or a self-regulatory organization.[5] Data on price and trading volumes must be publicly available. The regulators may amend exchange rules, and must approve all rule changes. Both SEC and CFTC have their own enforcement powers and staff.

The OTC market, by contrast, was largely unregulated until the Dodd-Frank Act. In place of exchanges, there is a system of dealers who stand ready to enter into derivatives contracts with all comers, whether the customers wish to hedge or speculate on prices rising or falling. Dealers are generally large commercial and investment banks that operate internationally—20 or 30 institutions account for virtually the entire market.[6] These institutions may be subject to regulation, but there was no direct regulation of their OTC derivatives dealings.[7] Neither dealers nor customers (also called end users) are required to report or make public OTC transactions: unlike exchange trading, very little information about prices, volumes, or individual positions is available either to the public or to regulators.

Although the exchange and OTC markets operated in very distinct legal environments, the products they offer are economically interchangeable. Traders routinely deal in both exchange-traded and OTC contracts, often as part of a single investment strategy. For example, a hedge fund might construct an investment position that included options on a basket of stocks (SEC-regulated), futures on stock indexes (CFTC-regulated), and OTC equity swaps (unregulated).

Market Trends: Trading Growth and Exchange Consolidation

In recent years, both exchange-traded and OTC derivatives markets have experienced remarkable growth. Table 1 below shows figures for 2000 and 2008 for a number of derivatives classes. The total of OTC contracts outstanding rose by 522% over that period, whereas the number of financial futures contracts traded on exchanges rose by 425%.

No single measure of market size can apply to both exchange and OTC markets. Because futures contracts are standardized instruments, the traditional measure of trading on the exchanges has been the number of contracts traded.

In the OTC market, the number of transactions is not a satisfactory measure, for several reasons. First, not all swaps are identical—a single trade here may represent more economic value than half a dozen trades elsewhere. Second, it is not always clear how to define a "transaction." Typically, a master swap agreement between two counterparties may be frequently amended as to the amount at risk by adding a new figure at the bottom of the contract. Over its life, a single contract may entail numerous transactions, depending on what happens to the underlying economic variables.

The standard measure of OTC market size is notional value, a concept that is explained in Appendix C. Notional value provides no information about actual swap payments; it is simply a reference number used in the calculation of those payments. It is possible to calculate a notional value for exchange-traded futures. An oil future, for example, represents 1,000 barrels of oil: the notional value of the contract is thus 1,000 times the current price per barrel. This figure, however, is of no interest to futures traders, because what concerns them is not the value of 1,000 barrels—which they will most likely never actually own—but the price changes that occur during the period that their futures position is open, which may be only a few seconds.

The Bank for International Settlements (BIS, the source of the data in Table 1) does publish a series on the notional value of exchange-traded futures based on financial variables (as opposed to physical commodities). The figure for such contracts in 2008 was $2.245 quadrillion, a figure that would seem to have few real-world analogues.[8]

In any case, Table 1 indicates that all categories of derivatives have grown extremely rapidly, by their separate measures. The expansion since 2000 is remarkable, though it has received relatively little attention in the press and academia. Some of the possible causes for this rapid expansion, and their policy implications, are discussed in the "Policy Issues" section of this report.

A consequence of the financial turmoil that has prevailed in world markets since 2007 has been a sharp downturn in derivatives activity. CME Group, the world's largest futures exchange, reported that it traded 23% fewer contracts in April 2009 than in the same month a year earlier.[9] BIS figures report a drop of 13% in the notional value of OTC contracts outstanding between mid-year 2008 and year-end (with credit derivatives declining by 27%).[10] Speculative losses and increased risk aversion may account for much of these declines. It remains to be seen whether long-term trends will be affected.

Table 1. Derivatives Trading and Positions, 2000 and 2008

Type of Instrument	2000	2008	% Increase
Exchange-Traded Derivatives (millions of contracts traded)			
Stock Options			
World	1,007	5,584	454
U.S.	673	4,187	522
Financial Futures			
World	1,045	5,489	425
North America	340	2,377	599
Physical Commodity Futures			
World	368	1,560	324
U.S.	160	560	250
Options on Financial Variables (other than single-stock options)			
World	596	4,852	714
North America	121	706	483
Options on Physical Commodities			
World	43	154	258
U.S.	36	142	294
Over-the-Counter Derivatives Contracts ($ trillions in notional value, at year-end)			
All OTC Contracts	95.2	592.0	522
Interest Rate	64.7	418.7	547
Foreign Exchange	16.9	49.8	195
Stock Index	1.9	6.5	242
Credit Derivatives	6.4 (2004)	41.9	555
Commodity Contracts	0.7	4.4	529
Other	12.0	70.7	489

Source: Bank for International Settlements, Quarterly Review and Semiannual Over-The-Counter (OTC) Derivatives Markets Statistics.

Notes: Comparable credit default swap data not available before December 2004.

Rapid growth in trading volumes has not been matched by a proliferation of derivatives markets. On the contrary, since 2000, there has been extensive consolidation among derivatives and securities exchanges, in many cases across national borders. Figure 1 below lists the top 10 global futures exchanges in 2000, and shows their current status. Only two of the 10 have not merged with other exchanges.

Notable changes include the merger of the three largest U.S. futures exchanges into a single firm, the CME Group, and the affiliation of the two largest European derivatives markets with U.S. partners. Although previous debates in Congress on derivatives focused on the economic impact of regulation, and the possible competitive disadvantages to U.S. markets of CFTC oversight, national borders may now be a less significant factor.

Factors driving consolidation may include increased competition, although the framework of that competition may no longer be U.S. versus UK versus continental European markets, but rather a battle by takeover for market share among global conglomerates. Mergers may produce economies of scale and cost savings needed to underwrite investment in new electronic trading technology, which is demanded by a customer base dominated by hedge funds, money managers, institutional investors, and financial institutions with global portfolios. Many exchanges (including CME and NYSE) have converted from mutual ownership to for-profit stock corporations, diminishing exchange members' ability to preserve the status quo. It has been argued that the emergence of a single, global monopoly marketplace for securities and derivatives is inevitable, and that individual exchanges feel they cannot afford to be left behind.[11]

Is monopoly possible? A key consideration is that the capacity to trade large volumes of financial instruments is no longer a barrier to entry. Cheap computing power has eroded the monopoly in trading infrastructure formerly enjoyed by the major exchanges. In this environment, regulatory licensing or registration becomes more important: a number of small regional stock and futures exchanges have been acquired by high-tech start-ups or joint ventures simply to provide a legal framework for launching a new electronic trading system.

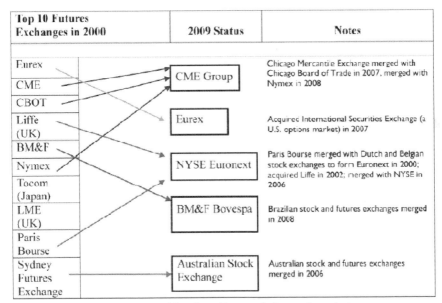

Source: Chart by CRS. 2000 ranking from Futures Industry Association.

Figure 1. Exchange Mergers Since 2000.

The OTC market may represent another source of cost pressure, assuming that there is significant demand for exotic customized instruments ill-suited to exchange trading. Market convergence is not limited to exchanges, but involves OTC participants as well. Most of the larger exchanges now offer clearing services for OTC contracts. As clearing of OTC derivatives becomes more common (either in response to market demand or legal mandates), further consolidation is likely. Major OTC dealers, like Morgan Stanley and Goldman Sachs, have participated in new clearinghouse ventures for credit swaps and other OTC contracts; given the right market conditions, firms like those would be fully capable of launching takeover bids for even the largest publicly traded exchanges.

POLICY ISSUES

Ten years ago, the consensus of U.S. financial regulators was that OTC derivatives were a beneficial innovation that had "transformed the world of finance, increasing the range of financial products available to corporations and investors and fostering more precise ways of understanding, quantifying, and managing risk."[12] A joint report by the CFTC, the SEC, the Federal Reserve, and the Treasury concluded that government regulation should not substitute for market discipline to reduce systemic risk, because "private counterparty credit risk management has been employed effectively by both regulated and unregulated dealers of OTC derivatives."[13]

A strong advocate of this position was Alan Greenspan, then chairman of the Federal Reserve. In a 1999 speech, he argued that regulation was not only unnecessary for OTC derivatives, but that even CFTC supervision of exchange-traded financial futures and options might not be in the public interest:

> The greater use of OTC derivatives doubtless reflects the attractiveness of customized over standardized products. But regulation is also a factor; the largest banks, in particular, seem to regard the regulation of exchange-traded derivatives, especially in the United States, as creating more burdens than benefits. As I have noted previously, the fact that the OTC markets function quite effectively without the benefits of the Commodity Exchange Act provides a strong argument for development of a less burdensome regime for exchange-traded financial derivatives.[14]

By 2009, many took a less benign view. The oil price shock of 2008 and the financial crisis that began in 2007 both raised questions about derivatives and their regulation. Neither episode is completely understood, but many observers believe that excessive speculation and lack of transparency in derivatives may have contributed to unwarranted volatility in energy prices and to the systemic fragility that allowed a slowdown in U.S. housing markets to trigger a worldwide crisis that has destroyed trillions of dollars in financial wealth and stalled real economic growth.

Derivatives and the Financial Crisis

There is little consensus about the relative importance of the numerous factors[15] that have been put forward as causes of the financial crisis, including the role of derivatives. It seems clear, however, that derivatives played some role in transmitting financial shocks from firm to firm and from market to market. Several aspects of derivative finance may be implicated:

- **Complexity.** At the peak of the housing boom, home mortgage loans were packaged, repackaged, and repackaged again into highly complex securities, many of which incorporated derivatives to increase yield or to obtain AAA bond ratings. As mortgage losses began to grow, no one could be sure what the real value of these securities was. As a result, the true financial condition of banks and other holders of these securities became uncertain; interbank lending slowed; and the conditions for panic were created.
- **Opacity.** In addition to the complexity of structured financial instruments, the nature of derivatives markets is to create a web of risk exposures among a wide range of markets and firms. Fears about insolvency in individual financial institutions were amplified by the knowledge that those firms might owe billions to derivatives counterparties—default of a single derivatives dealer had the potential to trigger cascading losses throughout the banking system. But no information about the extent or distribution of such potential losses was available, especially where unregulated OTC derivatives were involved.
- **Leverage.** In the post-2000 low interest rate environment, many market participants sought to boost investment returns through the use of leverage— supplementing their own capital with debt or derivatives. Since all derivatives trading is done on margin, a relatively small initial investment may generate a large return (or loss—see Appendix A). Thus, the losses in U.S. mortgage lending were magnified into much greater losses throughout the global financial system.
- **Excessive Speculation.** All the above factors combined to produce catastrophic losses at a number of systemically important firms that had amassed large speculative derivatives positions. A good example is AIG, which sold trillions of dollars in credit default swaps (CDS), and which had to be rescued by the government to prevent massive losses to AIG's counterparties, losses that could have greatly exacerbated the downward global financial spiral.[16]

Derivatives and the Oil Shock

In mid-2007, the price of crude oil stood at about $70 per barrel. Over the next 12 months, it climbed steadily, peaking at $145 in July 2008, and then plunged to $30 in December of that year. No hurricane, embargo, or other disruption of supply explained the price movements. It was possible to make reasonable arguments about the fundamentals of the energy industry that explained rising prices (demand from China and India, lack of spare production capacity, etc.) or falling prices (the global recession), but it was difficult to explain how both kinds of arguments could be correct within such a short time frame.

Absent any dramatic changes in physical oil supplies and fundamentals, many observers concluded that derivatives trading was in some way responsible for the price movements. Were hedge funds, oil companies, or others able to manipulate prices by buying and selling derivatives? Had financial speculation by pension funds and other institutional investors created a permanent upward bias in prices? Was unreported OTC trading driving the prices on the public Nymex exchange?

The CFTC testified repeatedly before Congress while prices were rising, consistently presenting the same message: there was no evidence of broad-based manipulation, therefore the market was simply reflecting the expectations of traders, as it is supposed to do.[17] This argument was not persuasive to many, who took soaring prices to be prima facie evidence of excessive speculation.[18]

On June 26, 2008, the House passed H.R. 6377 (110th Congress), which would have directed the CFTC to use its existing powers, including its emergency authority,[19] to curb immediately the role of excessive speculation in energy and to eliminate price distortion, unreasonable or unwarranted price fluctuations, or any unlawful activities that prevent the market from accurately reflecting the forces of supply and demand for energy. The measure was not enacted; the CFTC and others argued that moves to curb speculative trading would dry up liquidity and not necessarily stabilize prices.

Other 110th Congress bills addressed the OTC market—becausee the CFTC did not get regular information on OTC trades and U.S. firms' trading on foreign futures exchanges, some asked how it could be certain that manipulation was not occurring. In July 2008, majorities in both chambers voted to move two bills to increase oversight of OTC energy derivatives— H.R. 6604 and S. 3268—but the bills failed to obtain the votes needed for passage.[20] Many provisions of these bills are included in 111th Congress legislative proposals, discussed below.

CFTC Actions Regarding Energy Commodities

On July 7, 2009, CFTC Chairman Gary Gensler announced a series of initiatives to "ensure market integrity and efficiency."[21] The CFTC will hold a hearing on whether federal speculative position limits should be set by the CFTC for commodities of finite supply, in particular energy commodities, such as crude oil, heating oil, natural gas, gasoline, and other energy products.

In addition, the CFTC will make enhancements "in the near term" to its weekly Commitments of Traders (COT) report, which shows the number of contracts in open interest for all exchange-traded futures contracts and contains aggregate data on the number of contracts held by commercial and non-commercial traders. The CFTC will continue to use its special call authority to collect and report data from swaps dealers and index investors, many of whom trade in the OTC market.[22] Legislation before the 111th Congress—discussed below—would mandate that the CFTC take these and similar steps.

Derivatives and Crises

The association of derivatives with episodes of volatility and instability does not establish a causal relationship. Volatile markets are a prerequisite for derivatives trading—unless price volatility already exists in a market, there is no need to hedge and limited opportunity for speculative profits. Whether derivatives markets tend to exacerbate volatility is an unresolved question.

During 2007 and 2008, however, unexpected market movements took place against a backdrop not just of well-established and large derivatives markets, but at the peak of several years of very rapid growth in derivatives trading. Considering some of the reasons why derivatives trading was expanding and keeping in mind, with the benefit of hindsight, that the conditions for systemic crisis were developing simultaneously, certain tentative links between derivatives and the crises may emerge.

Rapid growth in derivatives trading during the 2000 through 2008 period can be attributed to several factors:

- After 2000, returns on stocks and fixed-income instruments were very low. Investors of all types—from traditionally risk-averse pension funds to high-risk hedge funds—may have turned to derivatives to increase yields. If so, the resulting increase in leverage may have contributed to systemic financial fragility. In addition, as already

noted, many of these derivatives-based strategies were both complex and opaque.
- The residential mortgage boom created a number of incentives for derivatives use. As large numbers of mortgages were refinanced at low rates, the holders of the mortgages had the option of using interest rate derivatives to hedge the risk of holding long-term, fixed–interest debt. As risky, non-traditional mortgages were packaged and sold as securities, derivatives were used to hedge interest rate and credit risks, to obtain AAA ratings, and to boost yields. Credit default swaps were employed both to hedge the risks of holding those mortgage-backed instruments, and to construct synthetic instruments that replicated the returns on mortgage-backed securities.
- Increased price volatility in the stock and commodity markets created incentives to hedge price risk and opportunities for speculative profits.
- The Commodity Futures Modernization Act of 2000 (CFMA) created statutory exemptions for OTC financial and non-agricultural commodity derivatives. CFTC regulation of these markets was thus largely precluded. The legal certainty produced by the CFMA may have stimulated trading in OTC contracts.[23]
- Financial innovation made possible the rapid trading of credit swaps and other exotic derivatives. Assuming that innovation surged in the post-2000 years, the ability of market participants and regulators to assess the risk of new instruments and strategies may have lagged the market by a greater-than-normal interval.

Together, these factors produced trends and incentives that may have helped set the stage for financial crisis and a bubble in commodity prices. Rising financial speculation created risks that were underestimated, perhaps in part because derivatives offered an illusion that risks were under control. The extent of speculation could have been masked by the proliferation of derivatives, many of which were complex, opaque, and hard to value, in addition to being unregulated.

It could certainly be argued that the mortgage bubble and energy price volatility would have occurred in a world without derivatives. The counter-argument, however, seems just as plausible, at least in the case of the financial crisis—that derivatives trading created such a degree of systemic fragility that if subprime mortgages hadn't triggered the crisis, another financial shock would have.

DERIVATIVES LEGISLATION IN THE 111TH CONGRESS

Title VII of the Dodd-Frank Wall Street Reform and Consumer Protection Act (P.L. 111-203) enacted sweeping derivatives reforms. The provisions of Dodd-Frank are not summarized here, but are the subject of a separate CRS report—CRS Report R41398, *The Dodd-Frank Wall Street Reform and Consumer Protection Act: Title VII, Derivatives*, by Mark Jickling and Kathleen Ann Ruane.

OTC Derivatives Markets

Requiring Exchange Trading of OTC Contracts

The Commodity Exchange Act (CEA) provides several exemptions that permit derivatives to be traded off regulated exchanges, free from most (or all) forms of CFTC regulation. A number of bills contain provisions that would narrow or eliminate those exemptions.

S. 272 (Senator Harkin) takes a sweeping approach—it repeals the sections of the CEA that exempt OTC derivatives and takes away the CFTC's authority to issue regulatory exemptions from the exchange-trading requirement. The bill would have the effect of abolishing the OTC markets in the United States, and would permit derivatives trading only on CFTC-regulated exchanges.

Other bills would remove the statutory exemption for OTC contracts based on energy commodities. H.R. 977 (Representative Peterson), H.R. 2448 (Representative Stupak) and H.R. 2454 (Representatives Waxman and Markey),[24] S. 221 (Senator Bill Nelson), S. 447 (Senator Levin) and S. 807 (Senator Ben Nelson) introduce new definitions of "energy commodity."[25] The effect is to remove energy commodities from the category into which they currently fall— "exempt commodities," defined as all commodities which are neither financial nor agricultural. Energy commodities would lose their current exempt status under Section 2(h) of the CEA, and would be treated the same as agricultural commodities—energy derivatives could be traded OTC only if the CFTC issued a specific exemption.

Requiring Clearing of OTC Derivatives

Several bills would require that OTC derivative contracts, such as swaps, be settled and cleared through a derivatives clearing organization. Clearing organizations—also known as clearinghouses or centralized counterparties—

are a standard feature of futures exchanges, where the clearinghouse stands behind all trades and guarantees payment. This means that traders do not have to worry about the creditworthiness of the opposite party (or counterparty), which facilitates rapid trading of contracts.

Because the clearing organization guarantees payment on all contracts, it has a strong incentive to prevent fraud or price manipulation that could cause traders to default. Thus, even when exchange trading is not mandatory, required clearing of OTC contracts would introduce a strong element of self-regulation into the market.

In addition, the clearinghouse is a central collection point for trade and position data. Because the clearinghouse collects margin payments to ensure that traders can meet their obligations, it has complete information on all positions. This allows regulators to share information on large positions, prices, and volume that reveals whether markets are functioning normally, are under stress, or whether manipulation or fraud may be occurring. The CFTC receives daily reports— called large trader reports—from the futures exchanges' clearinghouses on all positions that exceed a certain size.

In the OTC market, by contrast, a number of large financial intermediaries stand as dealers, who are willing to take the other side of their customers' trades. The dealers bear the risk of customer default, just as their customers bear the risk of dealer failure. Under current law, OTC dealers are generally not required to disclose market data to the CFTC or to other regulators. As a result, only limited information is available about the size of OTC positions, the number of transactions, or the identity of market participants.

H.R. 977 and H.R. 2448/H.R. 2454 would make clearing and settling through a regulated clearing organization a prerequisite for exemption from CFTC regulation. (The clearing organization could be regulated by the SEC or a federal banking agency, instead of the CFTC.) CFTC would be authorized to issue exemptions from the clearing requirement, for example, in the case of an OTC contract that was highly customized—clearinghouses manage risk by holding contracts that offset each other; this is difficult to do when contracts are not fungible and standardized. The bills specify that the CFTC may only exempt contracts where the counterparties meet financial integrity standards. Any contracts exempted from the clearing requirement would still have to be reported to the CFTC.

The bills would require clearing organizations to disclose certain position and trading data, either to regulators or to the public.

H.R. 1754 (Representative Castle) and S. 664 (Senator Collins) would require that credit swaps be cleared through a credit default swap trading clearinghouse designated by the SEC, in consultation with the CFTC and the Federal Reserve. The clearinghouse would be capitalized by swap traders to a level adequate to guarantee payments, and clearinghouse members could be assessed to maintain a default fund.

Increased Oversight of OTC Derivatives

In addition to—or instead of—requiring that OTC contracts be cleared or traded on exchanges, several bills would impose new reporting and recordkeeping requirements or otherwise increase regulatory oversight powers. S. 961 (Senators Levin and Collins) would repeal sections in commodities, securities, and banking law that prevent federal financial agencies from regulating swaps. The bill would authorize federal regulators—the CFTC, the SEC, and the banking agencies—to exercise oversight over swaps entered into by financial institutions, persons, or other entities subject to their regulatory jurisdiction. The regulators are authorized (but not required) to impose disclosure, reporting or recordkeeping requirements. Prior to taking action, the bill would require an agency to consult with the others. The bill includes a definition of "swap agreement," which specifies that a swap must be an agreement between eligible contract participants (as defined in the CEA) and that the material terms (other than price and quantity) must be subject to individual negotiation.

Reporting and Recordkeeping

Other bills authorize and direct the CFTC to establish reporting and recordkeeping requirements for certain OTC contracts. H.R. 977 would extend to the OTC market a version of the large trader reporting system that currently exists on the futures exchanges. It would (1) direct the CFTC to establish recordkeeping standards for OTC contracts exempted from regulation, and (2) require OTC traders to provide information about their positions upon a "special call" request for information from the CFTC.

S. 447 and S. 807 would apply recordkeeping and reporting requirements to energy and agricultural OTC contracts. S. 447 directs the CFTC to identify each large OTC transaction (or class of transactions) about which it needs information to detect and prevent potential price manipulation or excessive speculation. Participants in those transactions would file reports describing their large trading positions.

S. 807 authorizes the CFTC to issue "special calls" for information about exempted OTC contracts in energy or agricultural commodities that the CFTC determines to be appropriate to prevent manipulation, excessive speculation, or other disruption to market integrity.

OTC Position Limits

S. 447 would authorize the CFTC, based on information collected from OTC traders (see above) or following a major market disturbance, to impose limits on the size of OTC positions or the amount of OTC trading involving energy or agricultural commodities. CFTC's authority would be contingent on a need to diminish, eliminate, or prevent excessive speculation, deter and prevent market manipulation, squeezes, and corners,[26] ensure sufficient market liquidity, and ensure that the price discovery function of the underlying cash market is not distorted or disrupted.

H.R. 977 would authorize the CFTC to impose position limits on OTC contracts that it determined to be fungible with contracts traded on exchanges or other CFTC-regulated markets. Exercise of this authority would require a CFTC finding that such fungible OTC contracts had the potential to (1) disrupt the liquidity or price discovery function on a registered entity, (2) cause a severe market disturbance in the underlying cash or futures market, or (3) prevent or otherwise impair the price of a contract listed for trading on a registered entity from reflecting the forces of supply and demand in any market. This authority would cover all OTC markets, not just energy and agriculture.

H.R. 977 and S. 807 would require the CFTC to conduct a study of the efficacy, practicality, and consequences of establishing limits on the size of OTC positions in energy and agricultural commodities (H.R. 977) or physical commodities (S. 807). The studies would involve public hearings and would culminate in reports to the Agriculture Committees of the House and Senate containing recommendations on any necessary legislative actions or increases in CFTC resources.

Tax on OTC Derivatives

H.R. 3153 (Representative Larson) would amend the Internal Revenue Code of 1986 to impose a tax on over-the-counter derivatives transactions. The proposed tax rate would be 0.25% of the fair market value of the underlying property with respect to, or the notional principal amount of, the derivative financial instrument. It would apply to derivative financial instruments that are not traded on (or subject to the rules of) a qualified board or exchange.

Credit Default Swaps

Several of the provisions above would apply to credit default swaps (CDS), a form of OTC derivative.[27] In addition, several bills specifically address CDS.

H.R. 977 grants the CFTC authority—with the concurrence of the President—to suspend trading in CDS, if, in the opinion of the commission, the public interest and the protection of investors so require. The definition of CDS in the bill specifies that a CDS is not a security, and limits SEC jurisdiction over CDS to matters involving insider trading violations.

Two identical bills, H.R. 1754 and S. 664, would require all CDS to be cleared through a clearinghouse designated by the SEC (in consultation with the CFTC and the Federal Reserve). The bills would direct the SEC to issue rules to prohibit fraudulent, deceptive, or manipulative acts or practices in connection with CDS and to require that clearinghouses are (1) capitalized by participants to a level adequate to guarantee payments; and (2) authorized to assess members for a default fund. The bills also establish recordkeeping and reporting requirements for traders whose positions exceed a size to be determined by the CFTC.

H.R. 2448/H.R. 2454 would set new eligibility requirements for trading credit default swaps. Participation in that market would be limited to those who (1) owned the credit instrument that the CDS was insuring, (2) would experience financial loss if the credit event that triggers the swap insurance payment were to occur, or (3) met capital adequacy standards to be established by the CFTC in consultation with the Federal Reserve.

H.R. 3145 (Representative Waters) would amend the securities laws to prohibit credit default swaps and provide the SEC with the authority to regulate swap agreements that are based on securities. These provisions would apply to swaps entered into later than 180 days after enactment.

Enhanced CFTC Authority over Currently Regulated Markets

Following the 2008 run up in oil prices, the capacity of the CFTC to prevent excessive speculation or manipulation became an active legislative issue.[28] Several bills in the 111th Congress include provisions designed to improve the CFTC's oversight of futures markets.

Use of Existing Authority to Prevent Excessive Speculation in Energy

S. 1225 (Senator Sanders) and H.R. 2869 (Representatives DeFazio and Welch)—identical bills—would require the CFTC to use its authority, including emergency authority, to curb immediately the role of excessive speculation in energy futures or swaps markets within its jurisdiction and to eliminate any unlawful activity that prevents the market from accurately reflecting the forces of supply and demand for energy commodities. (A bill with similar provisions, H.R. 6377, passed the House in the 110th Congress.)

S. 1225 and H.R. 2869 also direct the CFTC to eliminate conflicts of interest that may arise when a single firm simultaneously trades energy derivatives, issues forecasts about oil prices, and operates oil assets.

Position Limits

Under current law, the CFTC has authority to set position limits for speculators on the futures exchanges. In practice, the CFTC has established limits for only about a dozen agricultural contracts, and delegates to the exchanges the task of setting limits for the hundreds of other futures contracts that are traded.[29] The limits take two forms: either a ceiling on the number of contracts that a speculator may control or an "accountability level"—a position size threshold beyond which traders must explain to the exchange why they have such a large position (and reduce the position if the exchange so orders).

Several bills would direct the CFTC to set position limits itself for futures contracts based on all physically-deliverable commodities (H.R. 977) or on energy and agricultural commodities (S. 447 and S. 807). H.R. 2448/H.R. 2454 requires CFTC to set position limits for energy contracts. Position accountability levels would not be a permissible substitute.

H.R. 977, H.R. 2448/H.R. 2454, and S. 807 would also require the CFTC to convene advisory groups (consisting of representatives of agricultural or energy producers, commercial purchasers of those commodities, speculators, and registered derivatives markets) to make recommendations regarding the appropriate levels for position limits.

S. 1225 and H.R. 2869 direct the CFTC to impose strict speculative position limits on bank holding companies and hedge funds engaged in energy futures trading.

S. 1412 (Senator Collins) would clarify the treatment of purchases of certain commodity futures contracts and financial instruments with respect to limits established by the CFTC relating to excessive speculation.

Reporting Positions of Index Traders and Swap Dealers

Another concern arising from the oil price experience of 2008 was that the CFTC's published statistics on futures positions might be understating the amount of speculation in the markets. In its Commitments of Traders reports, the CFTC publishes the number of contracts held by commercial and non-commercial traders. "Commercial" is traditionally thought to refer to hedgers; "non-commercial" to speculators. In recent years, however, a number of institutional investors, such as pension funds, have chosen to invest a part of their portfolios in commodities. They typically do this not by purchasing futures contracts on the exchanges, but by entering into an OTC contract that will track the performance of a published index of commodity prices. The swap dealer counterparty may then wish to offset the risk of the OTC contract by taking positions on the futures exchanges in the commodities comprising the index. Under current exchange and CFTC rules, swap dealers in this situation are able to qualify as hedgers and gain exemptions from speculative position limits. The CFTC reports such positions as "commercial."

It has been objected that this classification is incorrect, or at least confusing, because what the swap dealer is hedging is a speculative bet by the institutional investor. Accordingly, several bills would require the CFTC to disaggregate its Commitments of Traders reporting by breaking out positions held by swap dealers and "index traders"—investors following a passive, buy-and-hold strategy yielding returns linked to commodity price increases. H.R. 977, H.R. 2448/H.R. 2454, S. 447 and S. 807 all require the CFTC to collect and publish data showing the positions of swap dealers and index traders in the futures markets.

Bona Fide Hedging

A related issue has to do with the definition of hedging—traders who qualify as hedgers are generally not subject to position limits. A number of bills propose to narrow the definition of a hedger to exclude intermediaries who are hedging risk that arises from someone else's financial speculation, rather than transactions in physical commodities. H.R. 977, H.R. 2448/H.R. 2454, S. 447 and S. 807 include a new definition of "bona fide hedging." The definitions are not identical, but the common theme is that a transaction can be considered bona fide hedging only if at least one party faces risks arising from physical commodity dealings. In other words, a position taken by an investment bank to hedge the risk of an OTC contract with a financial speculator would *not* qualify, and the investment bank would be bound by speculative position limits.

S. 1225 and H.R. 2869 require that bank holding companies and hedge funds engaged in energy futures trading be classified as non-commercial traders (and subject to position limits).

The "London Loophole"

The "London loophole" refers to differences in the oversight of regulated markets in different countries. The UK counterpart to Nymex, the leading U.S. energy futures market, is ICE Futures Europe, which is based in London and regulated by the Financial Services Authority (FSA).

For several years, the UK exchange has been offering energy futures contracts in the United States, via electronic terminals. Ordinarily, an exchange offering futures contracts to U.S. investors is required to register with the CFTC as a "designated contract market," and to comply with all applicable laws and regulations. However, in the case of ICE Futures Europe, the CFTC has waived that requirement, by means of a series of no-action letters, on the grounds that since the UK market is already regulated at home, requiring it to register with the CFTC would be duplicative and add little in terms of market or customer protections.

With concern over high and volatile energy prices, there has been more scrutiny of ICE Futures Europe's activities in the United States. Can traders avoid speculative position limits by trading on ICE, in addition to (or instead of) Nymex? Does the CFTC receive the same information from ICE Futures Europe about large trading positions that could be a source of manipulation or price instability?

H.R. 977, H.R. 2448/H.R. 2454, S. 447 and S. 807 propose to close the London loophole, by making relief from CFTC registration requirements and regulation contingent upon a finding that the CFTC will receive from the foreign market information that is comparable or identical to what it receives from domestic exchanges and the foreign market is subject to anti-manipulation rules comparable to the CFTC's. H.R. 977 provisions apply to all commodities; S. 447 and H.R. 2448/H.R. 2454 to energy; and S. 807 to energy and agriculture.

S. 1225 and H.R. 2869 would revoke immediately each CFTC staff no-action letter that covers a foreign board of trade that has established trading terminals in the United States for the purpose of trading U.S. commodities to U.S. investors.

CFTC Resources

S. 447 directs the CFTC to hire at least 100 new employees. H.R. 2448/H.R. 2454 authorizes the CFTC to set and collect fees from registered clearing organizations at a rate calculated to cover the cost of derivatives regulation (with the exception of costs directly related to enforcement). Fee rates would be adjusted annually to make amounts collected approximately equal to the CFTC's budget authority for non-enforcement activities.

International Regulatory Coordination

S. 447 calls for the creation of an international regulatory working group. H.R. 977 and S. 807 call for a GAO study of the international regime for regulating the trading of energy commodity futures and derivatives.

Carbon Allowance Markets

H.R. 2454, the American Clean Energy and Security Act of 2009, proposes to create a cap-andtrade system for regulating emissions of greenhouse gases. It is likely that when and if emission allowances, offsets, and credits become available for trading in the United States on a large scale, a derivatives market in those instruments will emerge, as it has in Europe.[30] A number of bills address the regulation of that prospective market.

H.R. 977 and S. 807 envision trading of carbon allowance derivatives under CFTC oversight. The bills include identical language providing that derivatives based on "any allowance authorized under law to emit a greenhouse gas, and any credit authorized under law toward the reduction in greenhouse gas emissions or an increase in carbon sequestration" will not be treated as exempt commodities, but will be placed on the same regulatory footing as agricultural contracts. In other words, emission derivatives could only be traded OTC with a specific exemption from the CFTC.

H.R. 977 and S. 807 also direct the CFTC to enter into a memorandum of understanding with the Secretary of Agriculture which shall include provisions, consistent with section 1245 of the Food Security Act of 1985, ensuring that the development of any procedures and protocols for a market-based greenhouse gas program are properly constructed and coordinated to maximize credits for carbon sequestration.

H.R. 2454 (as passed by the House) provides for Federal Energy Regulatory Commission (FERC) regulation of trading in physical allowances. The CFTC would be the regulator for the allowance derivatives market, and would receive recommendations from an interagency working group including the Administrator of the Environmental Protection Agency and "the other relevant agencies." The working group would also report to Congress with any recommended legislative changes to ensure that markets are fair, transparent, stable, and efficient.

The interagency working group shall also make recommendations to Congress regarding legislative changes needed to ensure that allowance derivatives markets are transparent, fair, stable, and efficient.

The CFTC shall collect information and report periodically on the operation of the allowance derivatives markets.

H.R. 2448 specifies that the CFTC shall regulate trading of derivatives contracts based on carbon or greenhouse gas emissions or credits based on emission offsets or the production of renewable energy. Such "regulated allowance derivatives" (defined in the bill) are to be subject to the same degree of regulation as included energy transactions (defined in Section 3 of the bill). As noted above, this is the only section where H.R. 2448 differs from Subtitle E of Title III of H.R. 2454.

(As set out above, H.R. 2454 and H.R. 2448 also include provisions that apply to OTC and exchange-based derivatives in other commodities.)

Under S. 1399 (Senators Feinstein and Snowe), the CFTC would regulate both carbon allowance and carbon allowance derivative markets under a cap-and-trade system. The bill includes prohibitions against market manipulation, fraud, and excessive speculation; gives CFTC the authority to bring cases, open investigations, and use subpoena power to protect the marketplace; and requires that all trading of allocations and standardized allocation derivatives take place on "registered carbon trading facilities" and to be cleared by CFTC-regulated clearinghouses.

Registered carbon trading facilities would have self-regulatory duties, including market surveillance to detect manipulation, record-keeping and trade recording, enforcement of fair trading rules, and position limits. The registered facilities would also be authorized to order traders to reduce the size of their positions.

S. 1399 would require brokers, dealers, and traders to register with the CFTC as "registered carbon traders." They would have to meet professional standards; pass background checks; complete at least 20 hours of pre-registration education on trading ethics, rules, and laws; and pass a test approved by the CFTC.

The CFTC would maintain a centralized electronic position accounting system to monitor all large trader positions across multiple markets. The

CFTC would be authorized to collect trading fees to cover the cost of oversight.

OBAMA ADMINISTRATION PROPOSALS FOR DERIVATIVES REFORM

The Obama Administration on June 17, 2009, released a proposal for a revamp of the financial regulatory and supervisory system, which included a section proposing an overhaul of OTC derivatives regulation.[31] The stated goal of the Obama Administration plan is to bring all OTC derivatives under a coherent, coordinated regulatory framework that will improve transparency and market discipline in the OTC derivatives market.[32]

Key elements of the plan include the following:

- requiring that all standardized OTC derivatives are cleared through regulated central counterparties, and executed in regulated and transparent venues;
- increasing transparency in the OTC derivatives market, including developing a system for timely reporting of trades and prompt dissemination of prices and trading information;
- introducing reporting and record-keeping requirements on all OTC derivatives;
- preventing market manipulation, fraud and other abuses, including by amending the Commodities Exchange Act (CEA) and any securities laws to ensure the CFTC and SEC have clear authority to prevent and police market abuses;
- monitoring activities broadly in the OTC derivatives markets and ensuring they don't pose systemic risks to the financial system;
- strengthening regulation of OTC derivatives dealers and ensuring these products are not sold inappropriately to unsophisticated customers;
- bolstering the Federal Reserve's authority over derivatives markets infrastructure, such as clearing and settlement systems; and
- harmonizing the statutory and regulatory regimes for securities and futures.

The plan focuses on increasing transparency and standardization in the OTC derivatives market for all product types, and recommends that all "standardized" OTC derivatives be cleared by a clearing organization or traded on an exchange. But the plan does not specify what would constitute "standardized" as opposed to "customized" derivatives. Also, it does not mandate that all OTC derivatives be either traded on regulated exchanges or cleared through clearing organizations—only that as-yet-undefined "standardized" OTC derivatives contracts be cleared.[33] It does state that if an OTC derivative is accepted for clearing by one or more fully regulated central counterparties, then that should create a presumption that the derivative is standardized and thus would be required to be cleared.[34] The plan calls for Congress to amend the CEA and federal securities laws to require clearing of all standardized OTC derivatives through regulated central counterparties (CCPs).

The Dodd-Frank Act incorporated the basic framework of the Administration's proposals, with some significant changes. The act does not include the proposal's distinction between standardized and customized contracts, and it provides an exemption from clearing for commercial end-users.

Improving Transparency and Oversight

The Obama Administration plan also seeks to improve transparency in the OTC derivatives market, in terms of making aggregated market data available to the public, and seeks to improve price transparency in these contracts. The plan urges that CCPs and trade repositories be required to publicize aggregate data on open positions and trading volumes and develop a system for the timely reporting of trades and dissemination of prices. Also, CCPs and trade repositories should be required to make data on any individual counterparty's trades and positions available on a confidential basis to the CFTC, SEC, and the institution's primary regulators, under the Administration plan.

Some industry players reportedly wish to avoid price transparency, as they would lose money because wider bid-ask spreads from less-transparent prices generate larger fees.[35] The *Wall Street Journal* cited studies that found that an effort to improve transparency in the corporate bond market ultimately reduced bank fees by more than $1 billion a year.[36] Currently, the Depository Trust & Clearing Corp. (DTCC) collects information on most CDS trades, and releases aggregate data to the public weekly. DTCC recently sought to have its

Derivatives Regulation in the 111th Congress 55

trade repository overseen by the Federal Reserve, which could render it a regulated trade repository. Another financial information provider, Markit, currently publishes end-of-day prices on CDS linked to roughly 400 bonds. The *New York Times* recently reported that Markit Group Holdings was under investigation by the Justice Department for potential antitrust violations related to unfair access to pricing information for derivatives trades.[37]

In contrast to the OTC market, information on exchange-traded futures is widely available. For example, stock prices, real time trade, and price data are available for a fee from private vendors who contract with the exchange, whereas quotes a few minutes old are available free over the Internet.

The Administration also urges regulated financial institutions to make greater use of regulated exchange-traded derivatives (as opposed to currently unregulated OTC derivatives.) To improve both transparency and oversight, the Administration's plan urges Congress to amend the CEA and federal securities laws to authorize the SEC and the CFTC to impose record-keeping and reporting requirements, including an audit trail, on all OTC derivatives trades. Certain of the record-keeping and reporting requirements would be deemed satisfied when a standardized transaction is cleared through a CCP, or when a customized transaction is reported to a regulated trade repository.

Finally, the Administration plan also seeks to reduce fraud and manipulation in the OTC market, and to ensure that only suitably sophisticated participants are engaged in the OTC derivatives market. The proposal urges Congress to make any necessary changes to the Commodities Exchange Act and federal securities laws to ensure that the CFTC and SEC have clear authority to police fraud and market abuses, and to give the CFTC authority to set position limits on OTC derivatives, which have a significant price discovery function with respect to regulated markets.[38] Currently, the SEC relies on its powers under Section 10 of the Securities Exchange Act of 1934 to root out market abuses and fraud in the OTC derivatives market.[39]

The Administration plan also states that current limits on types of counterparties that can participate in OTC derivatives are not sufficiently strict, and notes that the CFTC and the SEC are reviewing participation limits, and will recommend how the CEA and securities laws should be changed.[40] Possible changes would include tightening the limits or imposing additional disclosure requirements or standards of care regarding the marketing of derivatives to less sophisticated counterparties, such as some small municipalities.

To make the OTC derivatives oversight regime more robust, the Administration also proposed the introduction of conservative capital requirements—namely, requirements more conservative than existing bank regulatory capital requirements for OTC derivatives—and also conservative requirements for initial margins on derivatives trades in order to hedge counterparty credit exposures in those trades. The plan urges that regulatory capital requirements for OTC derivatives that are not cleared through a CCP should also be increased for both banks and bank holding companies (BHCs).

Harmonize SEC and CFTC Oversight of Derivative Products

Another key component of the Administration plan is to eliminate jurisdictional uncertainties as to which types of derivatives products fall under which regulator, the SEC or the CFTC. For instance, under current federal regulatory guidelines, options on securities are regulated by the SEC, whereas security futures contracts on the same stocks are regulated jointly by the SEC and the CFTC, even though these products share similar characteristics. Other securities derivatives, such as stock index futures contracts (and options on those futures) are regulated by the CFTC. This type of overlapping and sometimes competing jurisdiction have consumed agency resources and impeded the growth of new products, as litigation established whether a derivatives product should be regulated as a futures contract or as a security. A stated goal of the Administration's plan is thus to eliminate jurisdictional uncertainty and to ensure that economically equivalent derivatives products be regulated in the same manner, regardless of whether the CFTC or the SEC has jurisdiction.

To achieve this, the Administration calls on the SEC and the CFTC to jointly develop consistent procedures for reviewing and approving proposals for new products and rulemakings by self-regulatory organizations (SROs), including, for example, SROs that govern CCP clearing organizations. The Administration plan also called on the SEC to harmonize its "rules-based approach" with the CFTC's somewhat looser "core principles" approach; and for the CFTC to toughen its approach to regulation to become more in line with the SEC approach. The plan calls upon the SEC, meanwhile, to recommend an expansion of the types of filings it accepts that should be deemed effective upon filing. It calls on the CFTC to toughen its standards to require prior approval for more types of rules. Currently, many CFTC filings are deemed effective upon filing.

The Administration calls on the CFTC and SEC to jointly complete a report to Congress by September 30, 2009, identifying all existing conflicts in statutes and regulations regarding similar types of financial instruments, and either explaining why those differences are essential to underlying objectives of investor protection, market integrity, and price transparency, or recommending changes. If the agencies fail to agree on their recommendations and explanations by September 30, 2009, then their differences should be referred to the new Financial Services Oversight Council, under the plan. The council would have to address the differences and make its own recommendations to Congress within six months of its formation.[41]

Other than in certain specific situations, the Administration has not yet made clear its position on the extent to which the SEC or other regulators, such as the Federal Reserve, should participate in the regulation of OTC derivatives. To some, any such role would represent a usurpation of the CFTC's jurisdiction, while others question whether the CFTC has the resources or the expertise to supervise the OTC markets in financial derivatives, where the major players are banks and other financial institutions.

The Dodd-Frank Act provides for some joint SEC/CFTC rulemaking, but the two agencies will continue to operate independently.

Additional Role for the Federal Reserve in OTC Derivatives Oversight

A key component of the Administration plan gives the Federal Reserve additional powers over the broader derivatives market, particularly in terms of policing the effectiveness of payments systems used to settle previously unregulated OTC derivatives transactions, which were largely bilateral private contracts. The Administration noted that during the financial stresses of 2008, regulators were extremely concerned that weaknesses in settlement arrangements for OTC derivatives and for tri-party repurchase agreements could be a source of financial contagion. The New York Federal Reserve has worked for several years with industry participants to reduce backlogs of unconfirmed trades in credit swaps. But the Administration stated that "progress was slow and insufficient,"[42] and that the Federal Reserve was forced to rely largely on "moral suasion" rather than existing federal authority to encourage systematic reforms.

To address these systematic risks, the Administration plan pledged to proposed legislation that would broadly define the characteristics of systemically important payment, clearing, and settlement systems ("covered systems"), and set objectives and principles for their oversight by the Federal

Reserve. Such legislation would give the Federal Reserve the power to collect information from any payment, settlement, or clearing system for the purpose of determining whether the system is systemically important.

If the system in question is subject already to CFTC or SEC oversight, then the CFTC or SEC would remain the primary regulator of the system. However, if that primary regulator does not already collect certain information, then the Federal Reserve would have the power to request such additional information directly from the system. The Federal Reserve would also have the power to impose risk management on these covered systems to ensure timely settlement. These risk management systems would be subject to regular, consistent on-site safety and soundness examinations by the CFTC or SEC, with the Federal Reserve having the right to participate in these exams. The Federal Reserve would also have the right to compel corrective action if risk management practices do not meet the applicable standards. The Fed would also have authority to require a covered system to submit reports on its risk management system.

Finally, the Administration plan proposes to extend access to the Federal Reserve's discount window to any of the derivatives payment, clearing, and settlement systems that the Federal Reserve, in consultation with the proposed Financial Stability Oversight Council, deems systemically significant. Such access should be for emergency purposes, such as enabling the system to convert noncash margin and collateral assets (such as real estate or other nonliquid assets) to liquid settlement funds, in the event that one of the system's participants fails to settle its obligations to the system. The Administration noted that many market participants had trouble obtaining liquidity from relationship banks by pledging or selling collateral during times of financial stress. This created the risk that a systemically important system could be unable to meet its obligations to participants when due because a bank that a participant relied on to provide such liquidity (or another market participant) would be unable or unwilling to provide the liquidity that the system needs. Extending access to Reserve Bank accounts and financial services and to the discount window for derivatives payment, clearing, and settlement systems is aimed at reducing this systemic risk.

Title VIII of the Dodd-Frank Act gives the Federal Reserve some additional authority over systemically important financial utilities, including clearinghouses.

APPENDIX A.
AN EXAMPLE OF FUTURES TRADING

An oil futures contract represents 1,000 barrels of oil, but neither party to the contract need ever possess the actual commodity. (Contracts may be settled by physical delivery, but in practice the vast majority are settled in cash.) When a contract is made today, one party (called the "long") agrees to buy oil at a future date from the other (the "short"). Contracts are available with different maturities, designated by expiration months, but the size is always the same. (In oil, a contract expires every month.) The price at which this future transaction is to take place is the current market price. Assuming the price of oil is $55 per barrel, the long trader is committed to buy at that price, and the short is obliged to sell.

Assume that tomorrow the price of oil goes to $60/barrel. The long trader now has the advantage: he is entitled to pay $55 for oil that is now worth $60. His profit is $5,000 (the $5 per barrel increase times the 1,000 barrels specified in the contract). The short has lost the identical amount: she is obliged to sell oil for less than the going price.

If, on the following day, the price goes to $65, the long gains another $5,000. The short, down a total of $10,000, may reconsider her investment strategy and decide to exit the market. She can do this at any time by entering into an offsetting, or opposite transaction. That is, she purchases a long contract with the same expiration date. Her obligation (on paper) is now to sell 1,000 barrels (according to the first contract) and to buy 1,000 barrels (the second contract) when both contracts expire simultaneously. Whatever price prevails at that time, the net effect of the two transaction will be zero. The short's position is said to be "evened out"—she is out of the market.

The short's decision to exit does not affect the long, who may prefer to ride with the trend. This is because all contracts are assumed by the exchange's clearinghouse, which becomes the opposite party on each trade, and guarantees payment. The ability to enter and exit the market by offset, without having to make or take delivery of the physical commodity, permits trading strategies based on short-term price expectations. While some traders may keep a long or short position open for weeks or months, others buy and sell within a time frame of minutes or seconds.

The exchange clearinghouse, which guarantees all trades, also controls traders' funds. Before entering into the trade described above, both long and short would have been required to deposit an initial margin payment of $7,763.

(The amount is set by the exchange; the figure is current as of June 4, 2009. Lower margins apply to hedgers and exchange members.) All contracts are priced, or "marked-to-market," each day. The long trader above would have had his $10,000 gain credited to his margin account, while the short would have had to make additional "maintenance" margin payments to cover her losses. It is worth noting that her two-day $10,000 loss represents more than 100% of her original investment, that is, her initial margin deposit of $7,763: the risks of futures speculation are high. When traders exit the market, any funds remaining in their margin accounts are returned. (Other transaction costs, such as brokerage commissions and exchange fees, are not refundable.)

Options on futures are also available for many futures contracts. The holder of an option has the right (but not the obligation) to enter into a long or short futures contract over the life of the option. The option will only be exercised if price movements are favorable to the option buyer, that is, if the underlying futures contract would be profitable. The seller of the option receives a payment (called a premium) for granting this right. The seller profits if the option is not exercised by the buyer. Appendix B has more information on options trading.

APPENDIX B. OPTIONS

In the futures contracts discussed in Appendix A, all gains by short traders create equal losses by long traders (or vice versa): futures trading is a zero-sum game. Traders who wish to limit their potential losses may choose to employ options, where gains and losses are not symmetrical. The key distinction between options and futures is that one party has the right, *but not the obligation*, to buy an asset in the future at a price determined when the option is purchased. There are two kinds of options: calls and puts. A call gives the holder of the options contract the right to buy an asset at a fixed price, while a put gives the holder the right to sell at a fixed price.

The price at which the underlying asset may be bought or sold is called the exercise price, or the strike price. An options contract confers the right to buy or sell for a specified period of time— each option has an expiration date.

On the other side of a put or call is the seller, or writer, of the option. The seller is obliged to buy or sell the asset at the strike price whenever the buyer chooses to exercise the option. In exchange for this right, the seller of the option receives a one-time payment, called the premium. The buyer's risk is limited to the amount of the premium—if prices move contrary to what the buyer expected, he simply lets the option expire unexercised, and the seller keeps the premium. On the other hand, the option buyer's potential profit is unlimited (just as a futures trader's is), because no matter how high or low the market price of the underlying asset may go, the option writer is obliged to buy or sell at the specified strike price.

The price of an option is reflected in the amount of the premium that is charged by the seller. A number of factors affect option prices: first, the relationship between the strike price and the current market price of the asset, which is called the intrinsic value of the option. If, for example, a put option on 100 shares of General Electric stock has a strike price of $14.00 and the current share price is $13.50, the intrinsic value of the contract to the buyer is $50.00 ($0.50 per share times 100 shares). An option is said to be "in the money" when the holder can exercise at a profit. If GE shares climbed to $15, the put option would be "out of the money," or "underwater," because the right to sell a $15 share for $14 is worthless.

In addition to intrinsic value, an option has time value. If the GE put in the example above is currently out of the money, there is still the chance that the share price will drop below the strike price before the option expires. Time value depends on the length of time to expiration and the price volatility of the underlying asset, which determines the probability of the option coming into the money during the life of the contract.

Options are traded both on securities and futures exchanges and over-the-counter. Underlying assets include stocks, stock indexes, futures contracts, currencies, interest rates, and physical commodities. Many OTC contracts include option-like features, including swaps, which are discussed in Appendix C.

APPENDIX C. SWAP AGREEMENTS

The OTC derivatives market includes a diverse range of instruments and contracts, but the building block of this market has been the swap agreement. The basic terms of a swap require two counterparties to exchange payments periodically. The size of one or both payments is determined by two factors: a notional principal (which is never actually exchanged) and some economic variable, most commonly an interest rate or currency exchange rate. To illustrate the mechanics and uses of swaps, consider the diagram above.

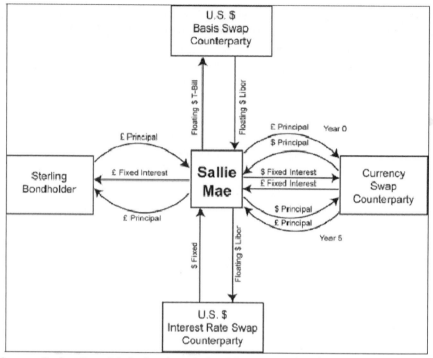

Source: Student Loan Marketing Association, Newspaper advertisement, 1992.

Figure C-1. A Swap-Driven Securities Issue.

The figure represents the phases of a single deal: the sale of a bond and the transformation (via swaps) of the financial obligations stemming from the bond. The process begins on the left, with a bond issue in London: Sallie Mae sells five-year, fixed-interest bonds, denominated in pounds sterling. However, Sallie Mae does not wish to be exposed to variations in the pound/dollar exchange rate. A currency swap gets rid of this risk: Sallie Mae swaps the entire principal of the bond issue (right side box), exchanging pounds for dollars at the current exchange rate, *which is then fixed for the life of the swap.* When interest payments are due to the bondholders, the counterparties exchange payments again; Sallie Mae receives the pounds needed to meet the interest payments, and pays dollars (at the fixed exchange rate). When the bond matures, the principal amount is again exchanged, in order that the bondholders may receive pounds. The currency swap allows Sallie Mae to fix the total cost of interest and principal repayment *in U.S. dollar terms.*

Next Sallie Mae wishes to avoid interest rate risk as well (i.e., the risk that market rates will fall below the bond's fixed rate). The bottom box represents the interest rate swap: Sallie Mae swaps a fixed rate obligation for a floating rate. Sallie Mae and the Interest Rate Swap Counterparty agree to exchange interest payments on a notional principal amount (which does not actually change hands) equal to the principal of the bond issue. The swap payments are set to coincide with interest payment dates of the bonds. Sallie Mae's payment is variable—determined by LIBOR (the London Interbank Offered Rate). In exchange, Sallie Mae receives a fixed interest payment that is equal to the amount needed to pay off the bondholders (after conversion into pounds via the currency swap above).

At this point, Sallie Mae has swapped its pound obligations for U.S. dollar obligations, and exchanged a fixed rate debt obligation for a floating rate. In the final step, Sallie Mae wishes to protect against the possibility of LIBOR (which determines Sallie Mae's payments on the interest rate swap) not tracking the U.S. Treasury bill rate, which is more relevant to Sallie Mae's domestic business. The top box shows the basis swap: Sallie Mae converts its floating rate LIBOR dollars to floating rate T-bill dollars on all interest payment dates. Sallie Mae makes payments based on the T-bill rate to its Basis Swap Counterparty in exchange for LIBOR-based payments, which it passes on to the Interest Rate Swap Counterparty. As the net result of the three swap deals, Sallie Mae converts a fixed-rate, pound-denominated bond into a floating-rate, dollar-denominated obligation. (Note however, that nothing changes for the original purchasers of the bonds: they receive fixed interest and principal repayment in pounds.)

These are basic, "plain-vanilla" swaps—two counterparties agree to exchange cash flows that are expected to fluctuate over the life of the swap. Derivatives become more complex when options characteristics are added to swap agreements, as when, for example, an upper or lower limit is set for one counterparty's payments, or when the exchange of payments begins at one party's discretion. The universe of derivative contracts is undergoing constant change as new contracts and exotic variations on old contracts are introduced.

APPENDIX D. GLOSSARY OF TERMS

This glossary has been compiled from several earlier CRS reports, from the CFTC website, and from other sources.

Arbitrage—A strategy involving the simultaneous purchase and sale of identical or equivalent instruments across two or more markets in order to benefit from a discrepancy in their price relationship. In a theoretical efficient market, there is a lack of opportunity for profitable arbitrage.

Artificial Price—A futures price that has been affected by a manipulation and is thus higher or lower than it would have been if it reflected the forces of supply and demand.

At-the-Market—An order to buy or sell a futures contract at whatever price is obtainable when the order reaches the trading facility. Also called Market Order.

At-the-Money—When an option's strike price is the same as the current trading price of the underlying commodity, the option is at-the-money.

Audit Trail—The record of trading information identifying, for example, the brokers participating in each transaction, the firms clearing the trade, the terms and time or sequence of the trade, the order receipt and execution time, and, ultimately, and when applicable, the customers involved.

Bank Holding Company—A business incorporated under state law, which controls through equity ownership ("holds") one or more banks and, often, other affiliates in financial services as allowed by its regulator, the Federal Reserve. On the federal level, these businesses are regulated through the Bank Holding Company Act.

Basis—The difference between the spot or cash price of a commodity and the price of the nearest futures contract for the same or a related commodity. Basis is usually computed in relation to the futures contract next to expire and may reflect different time periods, product forms, grades, or locations.

Beta (Beta Coefficient)—A measure of the variability of rate of return or value of a stock or portfolio compared to that of the overall market, typically used as a measure of riskiness.

Bid-Ask Spread—The difference between the bid price (an offer to buy) and the ask or offer (to sell) price.

Black-Scholes Model—An option pricing model initially developed by Fischer Black and Myron Scholes for securities options and later refined by Black for options on futures.

Board of Trade—Any organized exchange or other trading facility for the trading of futures and/or option contracts.

Boiler Room—An enterprise that often is operated out of inexpensive, low-rent quarters (hence the term "boiler room"), that uses high pressure sales tactics (generally over the telephone), and possibly false or misleading information to solicit generally unsophisticated investors.

Broker—A person paid a fee or commission for executing buy or sell orders for a customer. In commodity futures trading, the term may refer to (1) Floor broker, a person who actually executes orders on the trading floor of an exchange; (2) Account executive or associated person, the person who deals with customers in the offices of futures commission merchants; or (3) the futures commission merchant.

Bubble—Self-reinforcing process in which the price of an asset exceeds its fundamental value for a sustained period, often followed by a rapid price decline. Speculative bubbles are usually associated with a "bandwagon" effect in which speculators rush to buy the commodity (in the case of futures, "to take positions") before the price trend ends, and an even greater rush to sell the commodity (unwind positions) when prices reverse.

Bucketing—Directly or indirectly taking the opposite side of a customer's order into a broker's own account or into an account in which a broker has an interest, without open and competitive execution of the order on an exchange. Also called trading against.

Call—(1) An option contract giving the buyer the right but not the obligation to purchase a commodity or other asset or to enter into a long futures position; (2) a period at the opening and the close of some futures markets in which the price for each futures contract is established by auction; or (3) the requirement that a financial instrument be returned to the issuer prior to maturity, with principal and accrued interest paid off upon return.

Cash Commodity—The physical or actual commodity as distinguished from the futures contract, sometimes called spot commodity or actuals.

Cash Settlement—A method of settling certain futures or option contracts whereby the seller (or short) pays the buyer (or long) the cash value of the commodity traded according to a procedure specified in the contract. Also called Financial Settlement, especially in energy derivatives.

Circuit Breakers—A system of coordinated trading halts and/or price limits on equity markets and equity derivative markets designed to provide a cooling-off period during large, intraday market declines. The first known use of the term circuit breaker in this context was in the *Report of the Presidential Task Force on Market Mechanisms* (January 1988), which recommended that circuit breakers be adopted following the market break of October 1987.

Clearing Organization—An entity through which futures and other derivative transactions are cleared and settled. A clearing organization may be a division or affiliate of a particular exchange, or a freestanding entity. Also called a clearinghouse, multilateral clearing organization, clearing association, or central counterparty.

Close—The exchange-designated period at the end of the trading session during which all transactions are considered made "at the close." See Call.

Closing-Out—Liquidating an existing long or short futures or option position with an equal and opposite transaction. Also known as Offset.

Commitments of Traders Report (COT)—A weekly report from the CFTC providing a breakdown of each Tuesday's open interest for markets in which 20 or more traders hold positions equal to or above the reporting levels established by the CFTC. Open interest is broken down by aggregate commercial, non-commercial, and non-reportable holdings.

Commodity Exchange Act—The Commodity Exchange Act, 7 USC 1, et seq., provides for the federal regulation of commodity futures and options trading.

Commodity Futures Modernization Act of 2000 (CFMA, P.L. 106-554, 114 Stat. 2763)—the act that overhauled the Commodity Exchange Act to create a flexible structure for the regulation of futures and options trading, and established a broad statutory exemption from regulation for OTC derivatives.

Commodity Futures Trading Commission (CFTC)—The federal regulatory agency established by the Commodity Futures Trading Act of 1974 to administer the Commodity Exchange Act.

Commodity Pool—An investment trust, syndicate, or similar form of enterprise operated for the purpose of trading commodity futures or option contracts. Typically thought of as an enterprise engaged in the business of investing the collective or "pooled" funds of multiple participants in trading commodity futures or options, where participants share in profits and losses on a pro rata basis.

Corner—(1) Securing such relative control of a commodity that its price can be manipulated, that is, can be controlled by the creator of the corner; or (2) in the extreme situation, obtaining contracts requiring the delivery of more commodities than are available for delivery.

Counterparty—The opposite party in a bilateral agreement, contract, or transaction, such as a swap.

Counterparty Risk—The risk associated with the financial stability of the party entered into contract with. Forward contracts impose upon each party the risk that the counterparty will default, but futures contracts executed on a designated contract market are guaranteed against default by the clearing organization.

Credit Default Swap (CDS)—A tradeable contract in which one party agrees to pay another if a third party experiences a credit event, such as default on a debt obligation, bankruptcy, or credit rating downgrade.

Credit Event—An event such as a debt default or bankruptcy that will affect the payoff on a credit derivative, as defined in the derivative agreement.

Credit Rating—A rating determined by a rating agency that indicates the agency's opinion of the likelihood that a borrower such as a corporation or sovereign nation will be able to repay its debt. The rating agencies include Standard & Poor's, Fitch, and Moody's.

Credit Risk—The risk that a borrower will fail to repay a loan in full, or that a derivatives counterparty will default.

Day Trader—A trader, often a person with exchange trading privileges, who takes positions and then offsets them during the same trading session prior to the close of trading.

Dealer—An individual or financial firm engaged in the purchase and sale of securities and commodities such as metals, foreign exchange, etc., for its own account and at its own risk as principal (see broker). Dealers are said to "make a market" in commodities or financial instruments.

Delta—The expected change in an option's price given a one-unit change in the price of the underlying futures contract or physical commodity. For example, an option with a delta of 0.5 would change $.50 when the underlying commodity moves $1.00.

Derivatives—Financial contracts whose value is linked to the price of an underlying commodity or financial variable (such as an interest rate, currency price, or stock index). Ownership of a derivative does not require the holder to actually buy or sell the underlying interest. Derivatives are used by hedgers, who seek to shift risk to others, and speculators, who can profit if they can successfully forecast price trends. Examples include futures contracts, options, and swaps.

Derivatives Clearing Organization—A clearing organization or similar entity that, in respect to a contract (1) enables each party to the contract to substitute, through novation or otherwise, the credit of the derivatives clearing organization for the credit of the parties; (2) arranges or provides, on a multilateral basis, for the settlement or netting of obligations resulting from such contracts; or (3) otherwise provides clearing services or arrangements that mutualize or transfer among participants in the derivatives clearing organization the credit risk arising from such contracts.

Derivatives Transaction Execution Facility (DTEF)—A board of trade that is registered with the CFTC as a DTEF. A DTEF is subject to fewer regulatory requirements than a contract market. To qualify as a DTEF, an exchange can only trade certain commodities (including excluded commodities and other commodities with very high levels of deliverable supply) and generally must exclude retail participants (retail participants may trade on DTEFs through futures commission merchants with adjusted net capital of at least $20 million or registered commodity trading advisors that direct trading for accounts containing total assets of at least $25 million).

Designated Contract Market—the CEA term for a futures exchange.

Eligible Contract Participant—An entity, such as a financial institution, insurance company, or commodity pool, that is classified by the Commodity Exchange Act as an eligible contract participant based upon its regulated status or amount of assets. This classification permits these persons to engage in OTC and other transactions (such as trading on a derivatives transaction execution facility) not generally available to non-eligible contract participants, that is, retail customers.

Exchange—A central marketplace with established rules and regulations where buyers and sellers meet to trade futures and options contracts or securities.

Excluded Commodity—In general, the CEA defines an excluded commodity as any financial instrument such as a security, currency, interest rate, debt instrument, or credit rating; any economic or commercial index other than a narrow-based commodity index; or any other value that is out of the control of participants and is associated with an economic consequence.

Exempt Commodity—The Commodity Exchange Act defines an exempt commodity as any commodity other than an excluded commodity or an agricultural commodity. Examples include energy commodities and metals

Exercise Price (Strike Price)—The price, specified in the option contract, at which the underlying futures contract, security, or commodity will move from seller to buyer.

Forward Contract—A cash transaction common in many industries, including commodity merchandising, in which a commercial buyer and seller agree upon delivery of a specified quality and quantity of goods at a specified future date. Terms may be more "personalized" than is the case with standardized futures contracts (i.e., delivery time and amount are as determined between seller and buyer). A price may be agreed upon in advance, or there may be agreement that the price will be determined at the time of delivery. Forwards are generally considered cash sales not regulated by the CEA.

Functional Regulation—Regulatory arrangements based on activity ("function") rather than organizational structure. The Gramm-Leach-Bliley Act called for more functional regulation than in the past.

Futures Commission Merchant (FCM)—Individuals, associations, partnerships, corporations, and trusts that solicit or accept orders for the purchase or sale of any commodity for future delivery on or subject to the rules of any exchange and that accept payment from or extend credit to those whose orders are accepted.

Futures Contract—An agreement to purchase or sell a commodity for delivery in the future: (1) at a price that is determined at initiation of the contract; (2) that obligates each party to the contract to fulfill the contract at the specified price; (3) that is used to assume or shift price risk; and (4) that may be satisfied by delivery or offset.

Gamma—A measurement of how fast the delta of an option changes, given a unit change in the underlying futures price; the "delta of the delta."

Haircut—In computing the value of assets for purposes of capital, segregation, or margin requirements, a percentage reduction from the stated value (e.g., book value or market value) to account for possible declines in value that may occur before assets can be liquidated.

Hedge Exemption—An exemption from speculative position limits for bona fide hedgers and certain other persons who meet the requirements of exchange and CFTC rules.

Hedge Funds—Essentially unregulated mutual funds. They are pools of invested money that buy and sell stocks and bonds and many other assets, including precious metals, commodities, foreign currencies, and derivatives (contracts whose prices are derived from those of other financial instruments). Hedge funds are limited to qualified investors with high net worth.

Hedging—Investing with the intention of reducing the impact of adverse movements in interest rates, commodities, or securities prices. Typically, the hedging instrument gains value as the hedged item loses value, and vice versa.

Initial Margin—Customers' funds put up as security for a guarantee of contract fulfillment at the time a futures market position is established.

Institutional Regulation—Regulation that is institution-specific as contrasted with activity-specific (see functional regulation).

Interest Rate Swap—A swap in which the two counterparties agree to exchange interest rate flows. Typically, one party agrees to pay a fixed rate on a specified series of payment dates and the other party pays a floating rate that may be based on LIBOR (London Interbank Offered Rate) on those payment dates. The interest rates are paid on a specified principal amount called the notional principal, which is not actually exchanged.

International Swaps and Derivatives Association (ISDA)—A New York-based group of major international swaps dealers, that publishes the Code of Standard Wording, Assumptions and Provisions for Swaps, or Swaps Code, for U.S. dollar interest rate swaps as well as standard master interest rate, credit, and currency swap agreements and definitions for use in connection with the creation and trading of swaps.

In-the-Money—A term used to describe an option contract that has a positive value if exercised. A call with a strike price of $390 on gold trading at $400 is in-the-money 10 dollars.

Investment Bank—A financial intermediary, active in the securities business. Investment banking functions include underwriting (marketing newly registered securities to individual or institutional investors), counseling regarding merger and acquisition proposals, brokerage services, advice on corporate financing, and proprietary trading.

Leverage—The ability to control large dollar amounts of a commodity or security with a comparatively small amount of capital. Leverage can be obtained through borrowing or the use of derivatives.

Liquidity—The ability to trade an asset quickly without significantly affecting its price, or the condition of a market with many buyers and sellers present. Also, the ability of a person or firm to access credit markets.

Liquidity Risk—The possibility that the market for normally-liquid assets will suddenly dry up, leaving firms unable to convert assets into cash. Also, the risk that other firms will refuse to extend credit on any terms to a firm that is perceived as distressed.

Manipulation—Any planned operation, transaction, or practice that causes or maintains an artificial price. Specific types include corners and squeezes as well as unusually large purchases or sales of a commodity or security in a short period of time in order to distort prices, and putting out false information in order to distort prices.

Margin—The amount of money or collateral deposited by a customer with his broker, by a broker with a clearing member, or by a clearing member with a clearing organization. The margin is not partial payment on a purchase. In the case of futures, (1) *Initial margin* is the amount of margin required by the broker when a futures position is opened; and (2) *Maintenance margin* is an amount that must be maintained on deposit at all times. If the equity in a customer's account drops to or below the level of maintenance margin because of adverse price movements, the broker must issue a margin call to restore the customer's equity to the initial level. Exchanges specify levels of initial margin and maintenance margin for each futures contract, but futures commission merchants may require their customers to post margin at higher levels than those specified by the exchange.

Margin Call—(1) A request from a brokerage firm to a customer to bring margin deposits up to initial levels; (2) a request by the clearing organization to a clearing member to make a deposit of original margin, or a daily or intra-day variation margin payment because of adverse price movement, based on positions carried by the clearing member.

Market Risk—The risk that the price of a tradeable security or asset will decline, resulting in a loss to the holder.

Market Maker—A professional securities dealer or person with trading privileges on an exchange who has an obligation to buy when there is an excess of sell orders and to sell when there is an excess of buy orders. By maintaining an offering price sufficiently higher than their buying price, these firms are compensated for the risk involved in allowing their inventory of securities to act as a buffer against temporary order imbalances. In the futures industry, this term is sometimes loosely used to refer to a floor trader or local who, in speculating for his own account, provides a market for commercial users of the market. Occasionally a futures exchange will compensate a person with exchange trading privileges to take on the obligations of a market maker to enhance liquidity in a newly listed or lightly traded futures contract. In OTC derivatives, dealers make a market in swaps and other contracts.

Mark-to-Market—Part of the daily cash flow system used by U.S. futures exchanges and most OTC derivatives dealers to maintain a minimum level of margin equity for a given futures or option contract position by calculating the gain or loss in each contract position resulting from changes in the price of the derivatives contracts at the end of each trading session. These amounts are added or subtracted to each account balance.

Naked Option—The sale of a call or put option without holding an equal and opposite position in the underlying instrument.

Net Position—The difference between the open long contracts and the open short contracts held by a trader in any one commodity.

Netting—A means of reducing credit exposure to counterparties arising from multiple cash flows or obligations. Two forms of netting are widely employed in derivatives markets: payment netting and closeout netting. *Payment netting* reduces settlement risk. If counterparties are to exchange multiple cash flows during a given day, they can agree to net those cash flows to one payment per currency. Not only does such payment netting reduce settlement risk, it also streamlines processing. *Closeout netting* reduces pre-settlement risk. If counterparties have multiple offsetting obligations to one another—for example, multiple interest rate swaps or foreign exchange forward contracts—they can agree to net those obligations. In the event that a counterparty defaults, or some other termination event occurs, the outstanding contracts are all terminated. They are marked to market and settled with a net payment.

Notional Principal—In an interest rate swap, forward rate agreement, or other derivative instrument, the amount (or, in a currency swap, each of the amounts) to which interest rates are applied in order to calculate periodic payment obligations.

Open Interest—The total number of futures contracts long or short in a market that has been entered into and not yet liquidated by an offsetting transaction or fulfilled by delivery.

Operational Risk—The possibility that a financial institution will suffer losses from a failure to process transactions properly, from accounting mistakes, from rogue traders or other forms of insider fraud, or from other causes arising inside the institution.

Option—A contract that gives the buyer the right, but not the obligation, to buy or sell a specified quantity of a commodity or other instrument at a specific price within a specified period of time, regardless of the market price of that instrument. (See **Appendix B**.)

Over-the-Counter (OTC)—Trading that does not occur on a centralized exchange or trading facility. OTC transactions can occur electronically or over the telephone.

Portfolio Margining—A method for setting margin requirements that evaluates positions as a group or portfolio and takes into account the potential for losses on some positions to be offset by gains on others. Specifically, the margin requirement for a portfolio is typically set equal to an estimate of the largest possible decline in the net value of the portfolio that could occur under assumed changes in market conditions. In futures, this is also known as *risked-based margining*.

Put—An option that gives the buyer the right (but not the obligation) to sell a set quantity of an asset at a fixed price, called the strike or exercise price.

Reference Entity—An asset, such as a corporate or sovereign debt instrument, that underlies a credit derivative.

Repo or **Repurchase Agreement**—A transaction in which one party sells a security to another party while agreeing to repurchase it from the counterparty at some date in the future, at an agreed price. Repos allow traders to short-sell securities and allow the owners of securities to earn added income by lending the securities they own. Through this operation, the owner of the security is effectively a borrower of funds. The rate of interest used is known as the *repo rate*.

Security—Generally, a transferable instrument representing an ownership interest in a corporation (equity security or stock) or the debt of a corporation, municipality, or sovereign. Other forms of debt such as mortgages can be converted into securities. Certain derivatives on securities (e.g., options on equity securities) are also considered securities for the purposes of the securities laws. Security futures products are considered to be both securities and futures products. Futures contracts on broad-based securities indexes are not considered securities.

Security Futures—Futures contracts based on individual stocks, jointly regulated by the CFTC and SEC. Also called single-stock futures.

Securitization—The process of transforming a cash flow, typically from debt repayments, into a new marketable security. Holders of the securitized instrument receive interest and principal payments as the underlying loans are repaid. Types of loans that are frequently securitized are home mortgages, credit card receivables, student loans, small business loans, and car loans.

Self-Regulatory Organizations (SROs)—National securities or futures exchanges, national securities or futures associations, clearing agencies and the Municipal Securities Rulemaking Board are all authorized to make and enforce rules governing market participants. The respective federal regulatory agency has authority in connection with SROs and may require them to adopt or modify their rules. Examples of SROs in the futures industry include the National Futures Association (NFA), and the futures exchanges.

SPAN® (Standard Portfolio Analysis of Risk®)—As developed by the Chicago Mercantile Exchange, the industry standard for calculating performance bond requirements (margins) on the basis of overall portfolio risk. SPAN calculates risk for all enterprise levels on derivative and non-derivative instruments at numerous exchanges and clearing organizations worldwide.

Special-Purpose Entities (SPEs)—Also referred to as off–balance-sheet arrangements, SPEs are legal entities created to perform a specific financial function or transaction. They are intended to isolate financial risk from the sponsoring institution and provide less-expensive financing. The assets, liabilities, and cash flows of an SPE do not appear on the sponsoring institution's books.

Speculation—a venture or undertaking of an enterprising nature, especially one involving considerable financial risk on the chance of unusual profit.

Speculative Position Limit—In futures trading, the maximum position, either net long or net short, in one commodity future (or option) or in all futures (or options) of one commodity combined that may be held or controlled by one person (other than a person eligible for a hedge exemption) as prescribed by an exchange and/or by the CFTC.

Structured Debt—Debt that has been customized for the buyer, often by incorporating complex derivatives.

Swap—In general, the exchange of one asset or liability for a similar asset or liability for the purpose of lengthening or shortening maturities, or raising or lowering coupon rates, to maximize revenue or minimize financing costs. This may entail selling one securities issue and buying another in foreign currency; it may entail buying a currency on the spot market and simultaneously selling it forward. Swaps also may involve exchanging income flows; for example, exchanging the fixed rate coupon stream of a bond for a variable rate payment stream, or vice versa, while not swapping the principal component of the bond. Swaps are generally traded over-the-counter. (See **Appendix C**.)

Systemic Risk—The term "systemic risk" does not have a single, agreed-upon definition. Some define systemic risk as the risk an institution faces that it cannot diversify against. In other circumstances, systemic risk is defined as the risk that the linkages between institutions may affect the financial system as a whole, through a dynamic sometimes referred to as contagion.

Total Return Swap—A type of credit derivative in which one counterparty receives the total return (interest payments and any capital gains or losses) from a specified reference entity and the other counterparty receives a specified fixed or floating cash flow that is not related to the creditworthiness of the reference entity.

Volume of Trade—The number of contracts traded during a specified period of time. It may be quoted as the number of contracts traded or, for commodities, as the total of physical units, such as bales or bushels, pounds or dozens.

Warrant: An issuer-based product that gives the buyer the right, but not the obligation, to buy (in the case of a call) or to sell (in the case of a put) a stock or a commodity at a set price during a specified period.

APPENDIX E. LIST OF ACRONYMS

BIS	Bank for International Settlements
BM&F	Brazilian Mercantile & Futures Exchange
CBOE	Chicago Board Options Exchange
CBOT	Chicago Board of Trade
CCP	Central counterparty
CEA	Commodity Exchange Act
CFMA	Commodity Futures Modernization Act of 2000
CFTC	Commodity Futures Trading Commission
CME	Chicago Mercantile Exchange
DTCC	Depository Trust & Clearing Corporation
FCM	Futures commission merchant
FIA	Futures Industry Association
FSA	Financial Services Authority

ICE	InterContinental Exchange Inc.
ISDA	International Swaps and Derivatives Association
LCH.Clearnet	London Clearing House/Clearnet
LIFFE	London International Financial Futures Exchange
NFA	National Futures Association
Nymex	New York Mercantile Exchange
NYSE	New York Stock Exchange
OTC	Over-the-counter
SEC	Securities and Exchange Commission

End Notes

[1] Examples illustrating the mechanics of these contracts are set out in the Appendices to this report.

[2] Many futures contracts can be settled by making or taking delivery of a commodity, but in practice the vast majority are settled in cash.

[3] See Appendix A for an explanation of how this works.

[4] The Bank for International Settlements reports that 110.4 million financial futures contracts were open at the end of 2008, but that 5.485 billion such contracts were traded over the course of the year. This suggests that hedgers (who tend to keep positions open for longer periods of time) account for a much smaller proportion of trading than speculators, who tend to turn over their positions rapidly. (See *BIS Quarterly Review*, June 2009, Table 19, p. A103.) In Nymex crude oil futures, the open interest fell from 221,695 contracts at the end of the trading session on June 10, 2009, to 180,539, a difference of 41,156 contracts. Total volume for those days was 663,132 contracts, or more than 16 times the change in the number of open contracts. This indicates that the vast majority of trading is intraday, and not aimed at hedging long-term price risk. (Nymex data from Global Financial Data, a private vendor.)

[5] Federal securities and commodities laws permit the regulatory agencies to delegate registration and certain other functions to private groups, called self-regulatory organizations (SROs). In securities, the major SRO is the Financial Industry Regulatory Authority (FINRA). In futures, it is the National Futures Association (NFA).

[6] Testimony of Gary Gensler, chairman, Commodity Futures Trading Commission, before the Senate Committee on Agriculture, Nutrition and Forestry, June 4, 2009. (The figures appear in the oral version of his prepared testimony.)

[7] In addition, some regulated institutions house their derivatives dealings in off-balance-sheet subsidiaries, where capital and other regulatory requirements may not apply.

[8] Bank for International Settlements, *Semiannual OTC Derivatives Statistics at end-December 2008*, p. A108. The figure does not appear to include options on individual stocks.

[9] "CME Group Volume Averaged 9.2 Million Contracts per Day in April 2009," press release, May 4, 2009.

[10] Bank for International Settlements, *Semiannual Over-The-Counter (OTC) Derivatives Markets Statistics*, http://www.bis.org/statistics

[11] "Special Report: Battle of the Bourses," *The Economist*, May 27, 2006, p. 83.

[12] Over-the-Counter Derivatives Markets and the Commodity Exchange Act: Report of the President's Working Group on Financial Markets, November 1999, p. i (letter of transmittal).
[13] Ibid, p. 34.
[14] "Financial Derivatives," Remarks by Chairman Alan Greenspan before the Futures Industry Association, Boca Raton, Florida, March 19, 1999.
[15] See CRS Report R40173, *Causes of the Financial Crisis*, by Mark Jickling.
[16] See CRS Report R40438, Federal Government Assistance for American International Group (AIG), by Baird Webel.
[17] See, e.g., Written Testimony of Jeffrey Harris, chief economist and John Fenton, director of Market Surveillance, before the Subcommittee on General Farm Commodities and Risk Management, House Committee on Agriculture, May 15, 2008.
[18] Section 4a of the Commodity Exchange Act requires the CFTC to diminish, eliminate, and prevent excessive speculation, but the term is not defined in the act, nor is excessive speculation itself a violation. The impact of speculation on markets is an old question—most empirical studies find that speculation tends to reduce price volatility, without excluding the possibility that from time to time speculative price bubbles can develop even without deliberate market manipulation.
[19] CFTC's emergency authority includes the power to change margin levels or order the liquidation of trading positions.
[20] On motion to suspend the rules and pass, H.R. 6604 failed by the yeas and nays (two-thirds required): 276-151 (roll no. 540). Cloture on S. 3268 was not invoked in Senate by yea-nay vote. 50 – 43, record vote number: 184. For summaries of the bills, see CRS Report RL34555, *Speculation and Energy Prices: Legislative Responses*, by Mark Jickling and Lynn J. Cunningham.
[21] Statement by Chairman Gary Gensler on Speculative Position Limits and Enhanced Transparency Initiatives July 7, 2009. Available at http://www.cftc.gov/stellent/groups/public/@newsroom/ documents/speechandtestimony/ genslerstatement070709_b.pdf.
[22] See the "Reporting Positions of Index Traders and Swap Dealers" section below.
[23] Note, however, that regulated, exchange-based trading also grew very rapidly during the 2000-2008 period.
[24] H.R. 2454 (American Clean Energy and Security Act of 2009) incorporates nearly all the text of H.R. 2448 as Subtitle E of Title III, with only the section numbering changed. The exception is the last section, which covers regulation of carbon derivatives markets. The bills are referred to in this section of this report as "H.R. 2248/H.R. 2454," except in the material dealing with allowance derivatives, where they are discussed separately.
[25] Under current law, there are three categories of commodities—agricultural, excluded (financial), and exempt (all others)—subject to different degrees of CFTC oversight when they are traded OTC.
[26] See the glossary in Appendix D.
[27] See CRS Report RS22932, *Credit Default Swaps: Frequently Asked Questions*, by Edward V. Murphy and Rena S. Miller.
[28] See CRS Report RL34555, *Speculation and Energy Prices: Legislative Responses*, by Mark Jickling and Lynn J. Cunningham.
[29] The CFTC on July 7, 2009, announced that it would hold hearings on the need to impose speculative position limits on energy and other physical commodity contracts.

[30] See CRS Report RL34488, Regulating a Carbon Market: Issues Raised By the European Carbon and U.S. Sulfur Dioxide Allowance Markets, by Mark Jickling and Larry Parker.
[31] Department of Treasury, *Financial Regulatory Reform: A New Foundation,* http://www.financialstability.gov/docs/regs/FinalReport_web.pdf.
[32] Department of Treasury, Financial Regulatory Reform: A New Foundation, p. 6.
[33] Ibid, p. 47. For additional background, see also Department of the Treasury, Letter to Senator Harry Reid, May 13, 2009, accessible at http://www.financialstability.gov/docs/OTCletter.pdf.
[34] Ibid, p. 47.
[35] Serena Ng, "Banks Seek Role in Bid To Overhaul Derivatives," *Wall Street Journal,* May 29, 2009, p. C1.
[36] Ibid.
[37] Eric Dash, "Derivatives Are Focus of Antitrust Investigators," *The New York Times,* July 15, 2009, p. B1.
[38] Department of Treasury, Financial Regulatory Reform: A New Foundation, p. 48.
[39] The SEC has broad antifraud authority, extending into markets it does not regulate directly. While it can enforce antifraud provisions of the law in OTC markets, it has no authority to register OTC market participants or require them to disclose any trade information.
[40] Under current law, participation in OTC derivatives is limited to "eligible contract participants," defined in section 1a(12) of the CEA.
[41] Department of Treasury, Financial Regulatory Reform: A New Foundation, p. 51.
[42] Ibid.

In: Derivatives Reform and Regulation   ISBN: 978-1-61324-935-2
Editor: Aidan B. Lynch   © 2011 Nova Science Publishers, Inc.

Chapter 3

CONFLICTS OF INTEREST IN DERIVATIVES CLEARING[*]

Rena S. Miller

SUMMARY

The financial crisis implicated the over-the-counter (OTC) derivatives market as a source of systemic risk. In the wake of the crisis, lawmakers sought to reduce systemic risk to the financial system by regulating this market. One of the reforms that Congress introduced in the Dodd-Frank Act (P.L. 111-203) was mandatory clearing of OTC derivatives through clearinghouses, in an effort to remake the OTC market more in the image of the regulated futures exchanges. Clearinghouses require traders to put down cash or liquid assets, called margin, to cover potential losses and prevent any firm from building up a large uncapitalized exposure, as happened in the case of the American International Group (AIG). Clearinghouses thus limit the size of a cleared position based on a firm's ability to post margin to cover its potential losses.

As lawmakers focused on clearing requirements to reduce systemic risk, concerns also arose as to whether the small number of large swaps dealers in existence—mostly the largest banks—might influence clearinghouses or trading platforms in ways that could undermine the efficacy of the approach. Concerns about conflicts of interest in clearing

---

[*] This is an edited, reformatted and augmented version of a Congressional Research Service publication, CRS Report for Congress R41715, from www.crs.gov, dated March 22, 2011.

center around whether, if large swap dealers dominate a clearinghouse, they might directly or indirectly restrict access to the clearinghouse; whether they might limit the scope of derivatives products eligible for clearing; or whether they might influence a clearinghouse to lower margin requirements.

Trading in OTC derivatives is in fact concentrated around a dozen or so major dealers. The Office of the Comptroller of the Currency (OCC) estimated that, as of the third quarter of 2010, five large commercial banks in the United States represented 96% of the banking industry's total notional amounts of all derivatives; and those five banks represented 81% of the industry's net credit exposure to derivatives. The first group of Troubled Asset Relief Program (TARP) recipients included nearly all the large derivatives dealers. As a result of the high degree of market concentration, the failure of a large swaps dealer still has the potential to result in the nullification of tens of billions of dollars worth of contracts, which could pose a systemic threat.

A 2009-proposed amendment proposed to H.R. 4173, which passed the House, would have limited ownership interest and governance of the new derivatives clearinghouses by certain large financial institutions and major swap participants. Sections 726 and 765 in the final version of the Dodd-Frank Act mandate that the Commodity Futures Trading Commission (CFTC) and Securities and Exchange Commission (SEC), respectively, must adopt rules to mitigate conflicts of interest. However, it allowed the agencies to decide whether those rules include strict numerical limits on ownership or control. In the CFTC's proposed rules to mitigate conflicts of interest, published on October 18, 2010, and on January 6, 2011, the CFTC did choose to adopt strict ownership limits, along the lines of the Lynch amendment. The SEC's proposed rule, published on October 13, 2010, does the same.

This report examines how conflicts of interest may arise and analyzes the measures that the CFTC and SEC proposed to address them. It discusses what effect, if any, ownership and control limits may have on derivatives clearing; and whether such limits effectively address the types of conflicts of interest that are of concern to some in the 112th Congress. These rulemakings may interest the 112th Congress as part of its oversight authority for the CFTC and SEC. Trends in clearing and trading derivatives, and the ownership of swap clearinghouses, are discussed in the Appendix.

BACKGROUND

The financial crisis implicated the unregulated over-the-counter (OTC) derivatives market as a major source of systemic risk. In the wake of the crisis, lawmakers sought to introduce regulatory controls over this market, which many viewed as opaque and unregulated. A central element of the Dodd-Frank Wall Street Reform and Consumer Protection Act (P.L. 111-203) is a requirement that certain swaps be cleared by regulated derivatives clearing organizations (DCOs).[1]

Clearing is an institutional arrangement that helps protect against counterparty default. A DCO, or clearinghouse, clears and settles derivatives contracts between counterparties. This report examines how conflicts of interest in derivatives clearinghouses may arise, and what impact such conflicts could have on derivatives reform. It analyzes the measures that the CFTC and SEC have proposed to address such conflicts, and whether such proposed measures effectively address the types of conflicts of interest that are of concern to some in the 112th Congress. These rulemakings may interest the 112th Congress as part of its oversight authority over the CFTC and SEC.

Clearinghouses are a long-standing feature of futures exchanges. They exist to deal with a credit risk problem inherent in derivatives trading. Because derivatives are contracts linked to volatile prices, rates, or other variables, large losses may occur from time to time. Derivatives are bilateral contracts—typically, one counterparty benefits if the underlying price or rate rises; the other if it falls. How do the winners know that the losers will meet their contractual obligations? The clearinghouse guarantees payment of all contracts, offering an efficient alternative to requiring each trader to monitor the financial resources of other traders.

To ensure that it can make good on its guarantees, a clearinghouse requires all derivatives traders to put down cash to cover potential losses (called initial margin) at the time they open a contract, and requires subsequent cash deposits (called maintenance or interim margin) on a daily basis to help cover any actual losses to the position. If traders fail to answer a call for additional maintenance margin, their positions may be liquidated. The effect of the margin system is to eliminate the possibility that any market participant can build up an uncapitalized exposure (or paper loss) so large that default would cause the clearinghouse to fail. Initial margin rates are calculated to approximate the largest daily loss that a contract might experience under extreme market conditions. Margin rates are adjusted frequently to reflect shifts in volatility.

In addition to the margin system, members of the clearinghouse contribute capital to a fund to cover defaults, in the event that (1) the customer, (2) the broker, and (3) the clearing broker[2] are unable to meet the terms of a contract. No futures clearinghouse in the United States has ever failed.

Although the clearinghouse system was developed by private markets to deal with credit risk, posting margin to cover potential and actual losses has important consequences for systemic risk[3] as well. If a large derivatives trader fails, and the losses are not margined, its counterparties will be exposed to losses. There may be a widening circle of defaults, in the manner of dominos falling. This was a consideration that led the Federal Reserve and the Treasury to inject hundreds of billions of dollars into the American International Group (AIG) in 2008[4]—the fear that AIG's large bank counterparties would fail (or be perceived by the market as likely to fail, which can become a self-fulfilling prophecy if other institutions withhold credit).

Clearinghouses limit the size of a cleared position based on a firm's ability to post margin to cover its potential losses. If AIG had been required to clear its contracts and post margin, it would likely have run out of money long before its derivatives position reached a size that could threaten systemic stability. An important aim of the derivatives reforms in Dodd-Frank is to ensure that the scale of exposure that resulted in the downfall of AIG is not repeated.

Pre-Dodd-Frank Act Market Structure and Regulation

The different types of derivative financial instruments are used for the same broad purposes— hedging business risk and taking on risk in search of speculative profits.[5] Prior to the Dodd-Frank Act, however, these instruments were traded in different types of markets. Futures contracts are traded on exchanges regulated by the Commodity Futures Trading Commission (CFTC). Stock options are traded on exchanges regulated by the Securities and Exchange Commission (SEC). But swaps (and security-based swaps, as well as some options) were traded OTC, rather than on organized exchanges, and were not regulated by anyone.

The mechanism that exchanges use to deal with the issues of credit risk is a clearinghouse.[6] The process is shown in Figure 1 below: (1) two traders taking opposite sides of a contract (called long and short) agree on a transaction on the exchange floor or over an electronic platform. (2) Once the trade is made, it goes to the clearinghouse, which guarantees payment to both parties. (3) In effect, the original contract between a long and a short trader is now two contracts, one between each trader and the clearinghouse. The traders do not have to monitor the risk of counterparty default because the clearinghouse stands behind all trades.

In the OTC market, shown on the right side of Figure 1, the long and short traders do not interact directly. Instead of a centralized marketplace, there is a network of dealers who stand ready to take either long or short positions, and make money on spreads and fees. The dealer absorbs the credit risk of customer default, while the customer faces the risk of dealer default. In this kind of market, the dealers are expected to be solid and creditworthy financial institutions. The OTC market that emerged was dominated by two or three dozen very large and diversified institutions like JP Morgan Chase, Goldman Sachs, Citigroup, and their foreign counterparts. Before 2007, such firms were generally viewed as too well diversified or too well managed to fail. In 2008, their vulnerability was shown to be greater than previously assumed, and the question of their long-term creditworthiness now depends in part on whether the government would again intervene to ensure that their contracts are honored during a future crisis. (Title II of Dodd-Frank seeks to ensure that such risk is not borne by the taxpayer.)[7]

In the OTC market, some contracts required collateral or margin, but not all. There was no uniform practice: all contract terms were negotiable. A trade group, the International Swaps and Derivatives Association (ISDA), published best practice standards for use of collateral, but compliance was voluntary. The Dodd-Frank Act seeks to make standardized clearing of all forms of derivatives the norm, especially in transactions where the counterparties are systemically important financial institutions.

Source: CRS.

Figure 1. Derivatives Market Structure: Exchanges and Over-the-Counter (OTC).

The Dodd-Frank Clearing Reforms

Sections 723 and 763 of Dodd-Frank[8] require that all forms of OTC derivatives that meet the broad statutory definition of "swap" be submitted to a registered DCO for clearing, unless (1) no clearinghouse will accept the contract for clearing, or (2) one of the counterparties to the swap is an exempt commercial end-user.

Even with the exemptions, the law will result in trillions of dollars in derivatives transactions moving from the OTC dealer market into a clearing environment. At present some swaps are cleared voluntarily, but the volume of clearing is likely to expand manyfold when Dodd-Frank becomes effective.[9]

Although the clearing model has historically proved robust in the futures industry, there are concerns about a sudden upsurge in the volume of swaps clearing. Unlike futures, many swaps are customized and complex contracts. The value of most futures contracts is linked directly to the price of a single underlying commodity, rate, or index, or a ratio. To calculate the potential risk from a futures position, one simply needs to estimate the volatility of the underlying interest. With swaps, the relationship between changes in the underlying variables and the value of the contract may not be linear. Also unlike futures, swaps do not have standardized maturity dates. Some swap markets may have low trading volume, but very large contract sizes. Because of these distinctions, pricing risk in swaps may be more complex and prone to error than pricing risk in futures.

Difficulty in pricing swaps could be a source of systemic risk. If derivatives risk is concentrated in a handful of clearinghouses, failure to price risk correctly (and set margins accordingly) could cause a clearinghouse to fail during a market crisis, potentially with systemic repercussions. Rather than simply mandate clearing, Dodd-Frank includes a number of safeguards intended to mitigate the risks in swaps clearing.

Safeguards for Swaps Clearing

Congress addressed two major concerns about swaps clearing in the Dodd-Frank Act: risk management and control and governance of clearinghouses. Before a swap can be cleared, several hurdles must be crossed:

- **A clearinghouse must be willing to accept the swap for clearing.** Under Dodd-Frank, regulators may not force DCOs to clear swaps.[10]

Thus, if clearinghouses deem a particular product too risky for clearing, they do not have to accept it.
- **The regulators must approve the swap for clearing.** If the CFTC or SEC believes that a DCO lacks the technical expertise or financial resources to manage the risk in clearing a swap or class of swaps, the swap may not be cleared.
- **DCOs must meet regulatory and statutory standards.** Sections 725 and 762 of the Dodd-Frank Act set out sets of core principles that DCOs must meet as a condition of registration. These include having adequate financial, managerial, and operational resources; appropriate standards for accepting swaps for clearing; the ability to manage risk; and risk control mechanisms that limit exposure to losses that could disrupt clearing operations or spill over onto non-defaulting market participants.

From one perspective, enforcing the above provisions of the law may not require a heavy regulatory hand. DCOs have strong economic incentives to make sure that (1) market participants post enough margin to cover their individual losses; (2) the exchange membership as a whole has sufficient capital to mutualize losses should a member institution or customer fail; (3) that the DCO can net out its position through offsetting counterparty positions, so that it is not at risk from market price fluctuations; and (4) that trades are transparent enough to enable effective monitoring of emerging risks to the trading network. The incentives of clearinghouses to stay in business and the incentives of regulators to prevent financial instability appear to be aligned.

However, Congress and regulators have identified potential counter-incentives that may lead DCOs to act in a way that increases systemic risk. In theory, there may be short-term commercial advantages to behavior that works against stability. In particular, attention focused on the possibility that the handful of dealer banks that dominated the OTC derivatives market could weaken the Dodd-Frank reforms by exercising undue influence over the clearing process.

CONFLICTS OF INTEREST IN CLEARING

As lawmakers focused on clearing, concerns arose as to whether the small number of large swaps dealers in existence might influence clearinghouses or trading platforms in ways that could undermine the potential efficacy of clearing in mitigating systemic risk. Could powerful large banks that were both swap dealers and clearing members in a derivatives clearinghouse influence the clearinghouse not to clear certain OTC products in order to maintain the status quo in the lucrative swaps dealing business? Could they influence a clearinghouse to set margin insufficiently low for certain OTC swaps for which they dominated the market? Could they set capital requirements for clearing members unnecessarily high to keep smaller banks out of the OTC market, limit competition, and maintain higher fees?

The Dodd-Frank Act directs the CFTC and SEC to identify the nature and sources of any conflicts of interest that relate to the voting interests in, or governance of, a DCO that may interfere with achieving the policy objectives of the clearing mandate. The SEC has identified three types of conflicts of interest:[11]

- First, DCO members could limit access to the clearing agency. This can occur either by restricting direct participation in the clearing agency, or restricting indirect access by controlling the ability of non-members to enter into correspondent clearing arrangements.
- Second, DCO members could limit the scope of products eligible for clearing, particularly if there is a strong economic incentive to keep a product traded in the OTC market, where there is less transparency and dealer spreads between bid and ask prices are likely to be wider.
- Third, DCO members could use their influence to lower the risk management controls of a clearinghouse to reduce the amount of collateral they would be required to contribute and liquidity resources they would have to expend as margin or guaranty fund to the security-based swap clearing agency.

The CFTC identifies similar potential conflicts of interest. First, in determining whether a swap contract is capable of being cleared; second, in determining the minimum criteria that an entity must meet to become a clearinghouse member; and third, in determining whether a particular entity satisfies the membership criteria.[12] Others have raised a related issue: the possibility of a "race to the bottom" if competing clearinghouses cut margin requirements to imprudent levels in search of market share. While this strategy might jeopardize the long-term survival of the DCO, it could generate short-term profits from clearing fees.

These concerns largely reflect the possibility that large derivatives dealers could come to dominate swaps clearing and essentially seek to preserve the status quo ante of the OTC market. Parts of the concern may appear counterintuitive—why would a clearinghouse refuse to clear?— or may be addressed elsewhere—regulators have authority to require that access to DCOs be open and nondiscriminatory. Some may find improbable the scenario of clearinghouse members deliberately setting capital and margin standards too low. Nonetheless, the issue of concentrated ownership and control of derivatives clearinghouses was a subject of intense debate in the 111th Congress and was addressed in different ways by various iterations of the financial reform legislation that became the Dodd-Frank Act.

Legislative Approaches to Conflicts of Interest

As concerns about the structure of clearinghouses arose in 2009, Representative Stephen F. Lynch proposed an amendment to H.R. 4173, which would have restricted ownership interest and governance of the new derivatives clearinghouses by certain large financial institutions and major swap participants.[13] The Lynch amendment set a 20% limit on the collective ownership of clearing and trading entities by so-called "restricted owners," which included swap dealers, major swap participants, and their security-based swap counterparts, to prevent conflicts of interest. The Lynch amendment was adopted by the House by a vote of 228-202.

The Senate, however, did not take the approach of the Lynch amendment in its version of H.R. 4173. The provisions of the Lynch amendment were ultimately not included in the conference report on H.R. 4173, but the report did, in Sections 726 and 765, include language related to conflicts of interest in swaps clearinghouses. The final version of Dodd-Frank does not impose statutory restrictions on DCO ownership, but does require the regulators to make rules to mitigate conflicts of interest, which could include numerical limits on control and ownership of clearinghouses.

An examination of the legislative history documents accompanying H.R. 4173 does not reveal a rationale for the conferees omitting the language of the Lynch amendment in their final report, or in choosing to include the conflict of interest provisions of Sections 726 and 765. During conference deliberations on H.R. 4173, the House conferees reportedly proposed legislative language to their Senate counterparts which included the language of the Lynch amendment.[14] In doing so, Conference Chairman Representative Barney Frank stated that he and the House conferees viewed the Lynch language as "very important."[15]

Senate conferees reportedly rejected portions of the House offer, including the Lynch language.[16] Instead of setting strict ownership caps, they opted to require regulators to write rules to mitigate conflicts of interest, which could include numerical limits on the control and ownership of clearinghouses, exchanges and other entities.[17] The House ultimately accepted the Senate position. In a June 30, 2010, colloquy on the House floor, Representatives Lynch and Frank clarified the intent of Sections 726 and 765 of the conference report, including making clear that the rulemaking envisioned by the sections was mandatory, not to be done at the discretion of the CFTC and the SEC.[18]

In the final Dodd-Frank Act, Sections 726 and 765 mandate that the CFTC and SEC, respectively, must adopt rules to mitigate conflicts of interest; but leave it to the agencies themselves to decide whether those rules should include strict numerical limits on ownership or control.

Regulatory Proposals

Both the CFTC and the SEC published proposed rules on conflicts of interest in October 2010. The rules included similar percentage limits on ownership and voting control of DCOs. In addition, the releases contain a number of proposed requirements that DCOs have governance structures to insulate them from control by large financial institutions.

In the CFTC's proposed rules to mitigate conflicts of interest, published on October 18, 2010,[19] and on January 6, 2011,[20] the CFTC did choose to propose strict ownership limits, along the lines of the Lynch amendment. The SEC's proposed rules also adopt such limits.[21] The CFTC and SEC propose to limit the amount of voting equity or voting power that certain "enumerated entities"[22] may own or exercise, individually or collectively, with respect to DCOs.[23] The enumerated entities are those set forth in the statute:[24] (1) bank holding companies with total consolidated assets over $50 billion and their affiliates, (2) nonbank financial companies supervised by the Board of Governors of the Federal Reserve System and affiliates of such companies, (3) swap dealers and associated persons of swap dealers, and (4) major swap participants (MSPs) and associated persons of MSPs.

Under the proposed rules, a DCO may choose to comply with either of two alternative sets of ownership and control limits:

Option One. A DCO member may not individually:

- beneficially own more than 20% of any class of voting equity in the DCO; or
- directly or indirectly vote an interest exceeding 20% of the voting power of any class of equity interest in the DCO.

In addition, enumerated entities—regardless of DCO membership—may not collectively:

- beneficially own more than 40% of any class of voting equity in a DCO; or
- directly or indirectly vote an interest exceeding 40% of the voting power of any class of equity interest in the DCO.

Option Two. A DCO member or enumerated entity regardless of DCO membership may not:

- own more than 5% of any class of voting equity in the DCO; or directly or indirectly vote an interest exceeding 5% of the voting power of any class of equity interest in the DCO.

Some opponents of the proposed rules argue that mandating a more fragmented ownership structure for DCOs could lead them to be undercapitalized.[25] This is risky for DCOs, they argue, which would benefit in times of crisis from the large amounts of capital required to be held by the current large swap dealers who already dominate the swaps market—most of them big banks. If regulators restrict the ownership of DCOs by such large banks, they argue, then smaller and less well-capitalized entities will have to make up the rest of the clearing members, thereby reducing both critical swap-market expertise and access to capital on the part of the DCO. They also argue that limiting the ownership of large banks who are the major swap dealers would also limit the crucial expertise on swaps that DCOs need in order to accurately assess the riskiness of various derivatives, and to decide whether to clear them, and if so, how to set margin requirements accurately.

One of the five CFTC commissioners, Jill E. Sommers, voted against the rule proposal, arguing that the voting equity restrictions are not necessary or appropriate to mitigate the perceived conflicts and may stifle competition by preventing the formation of new swaps trading and clearing firms. Commissioner Sommers also noted that the European Commission rejected ownership limitations.[26]

The CFTC previously addressed a similar kind of structural conflict of interest in a 2007 final rule addressing conflicts of interest in futures exchanges (designated contract markets, or DCMs).[27] In the regulatory framework prior to the Dodd-Frank Act, DCMs were subject to flexible "core principles," including core principle 15 regarding conflicts of interest, instead of more prescriptive rules. Title VII of the Dodd-Frank Act retains various DCM core principles with certain additions and changes (and renumbers 15 to 16). Core principle 16 requires DCMs to establish and enforce rules (1) to minimize conflicts of interest in the decision-making process of the DCM, and (2) to establish a process for resolving such conflicts of interest.[28] The CFTC's 2007 final rule adopted "acceptable practices" for minimizing conflicts of interest pursuant to the DCM core principle. The acceptable practices address conflicts of interest within DCMs as they transform from member-owned, not-for-profit entities into diverse enterprises with a variety of business models and ownership structures.[29] The CFTC indicated that the presence of potentially conflicting demands, that is, regulatory authority coupled with commercial incentives to misuse such authority, constitutes a new structural conflict of interest.[30] The Dodd-Frank Act also contains a revised set of core principles for DCOs,[31] including management of conflicts of interest.

In addition to the numerical ownership restrictions, the CFTC and SEC propose to require certain governance structures to prevent conflicts of interest in DCOs. These include

- a requirement that 35% of DCO boards of directors (or at least two board members) be independent directors;[32]
- a requirement that 35% of any committee with authority to act on behalf of the board of directors regarding management of a DCO must consist of independent directors; and
- a requirement that each DCO have a Risk Management Committee with a composition of 35% independent directors with sufficient expertise in, among other things, clearing services.

Additionally, the CFTC rules include

- the prohibition of a DCO from being operated by another entity unless such entity agrees to comport with such requirements in the same manner as the DCO; and
- the prohibition of a DCO from permitting itself to be operated by any entity unless such entity agrees to subject (1) its officers, directors,

employees, and agents to CFTC or SEC authority, and (2) makes its books and records available to the CFTC or SEC for inspection.

Opponents of the Rule

Some fear that the conflicts of interest rules will harm competition by limiting entry of new DCOs, SEFs, and DCMs to the market.[33] They warn that the rule will hinder the ability of new DCOs to find investors who will devote their time, expertise, and capital if they know they are not able to retain more than a 20% voting equity.[34] Without basic governance rights, these critics argue, investors would lose control over commercial interests (which would include revenue policy and intellectual property). At the same time, they argue, it will force existing DCOs to find ways to replace the portion of their capital that is currently funded by "enumerated entities." They protest that, in effect, the rule will limit trading and clearing options for market participants, limit competition, and cause market uncertainty—as traders question the security of funds for existing DCOs.[35]

Additionally, some of the industry's largest banks argue that a limit on aggregate ownership of DCOs (the second option of the CFTC's proposed rule) can cause conflicts of interest amongst non-members, also potentially exacerbating systemic risk.[36] They fear that non-member owners will not possess the appropriate expertise to manage their entities' decisions and they will not share the same principles that prioritize risk management over return on investments. In most clearinghouse structures, they explain, non-member owners may not share the same risk exposure as members when a counterparty defaults, and this can compel them to take greater risks when making important business decisions.

Meanwhile some commenters have noted that the rule will be ineffective for mitigating conflicts of interest amongst members and non-members. They claim that putting a cap on ownership rights does not restrict voting rights—and thus the influence—that a dealer might wield over a DCO.[37] For this reason, they recommend that the regulatory agencies weigh the realistic costs of the ownership rule against its supposed benefits.

Proponents of the Rule

Proponents of the rule, on the other hand, underscore the risk that the system and the DCOs, SEFs, and DCMs would face if allowed to operate by only a handful of large firms.[38] The main problem with allowing these entities to remain unrestricted in ownership and voting rights, they argue, is such entities will unlikely demand sufficient collateral to control risk. We saw the same large banks fail to require sufficient collateral from AIG in the lead-up to the financial crisis, they explain; and as a result of the "undercapitalization" of these banks, billions of dollars were needed from Treasury, the Federal Reserve, and the FDIC to prevent widespread default. There is therefore no guarantee that the financial industry's largest banks would require the appropriate level of collateral when running their clearinghouses, these commenters argue. Without the proposed SEC and CFTC rule, they believe the system would be vulnerable to the same risk that was present before the crisis, this time with concentrated risk among the nation's largest clearinghouses.

Then, there is also concern that the agencies have not gone far enough in limiting dealers from gaining monopolistic control over clearinghouses, SEFs, and exchanges.[39] They argue that the purpose of Dodd-Frank—to limit the dominance of the five large banks in the OTC market, and to promote greater competition amongst market participants—is not being fulfilled by the issuance of a 5% ownership cap by any one entity or broker. The problem, they explain, is that brokers will still be able to "band together" to collectively own the majority of DCO, SEF, and DCM operations, which the large banks are likely to do since they share similar interests. After forming these inconspicuous cohorts, they argue, the big banks will be able to dictate the decision making in their respective exchanges, clearinghouses, and execution facilities. Because of this potential loophole (i.e., the fact that the rule does not mandate a limit on aggregate ownership), these critics encourage the CFTC and the SEC to consider issuing stronger restrictions on collective ownership that will better ensure that no one entity or class of entities will dominate DCOs.

APPENDIX. CURRENT OWNERSHIP OF SWAP CLEARINGHOUSES

Over the past decade, most exchanges and clearinghouses have become "vertically integrated," meaning the DCOs have become subsidiaries or divisions within certain exchanges.[40] Throughout the United States and Europe, there are three main clearinghouse-exchanges that clear and trade OTC derivatives: the Chicago Mercantile Exchange Group (CME), the IntercontinentalExchange (ICE), and LCH.Clearnet. The ownership structure and operations of these clearinghouses and exchanges will likely be affected by Dodd-Frank and the CFTC's proposed rules.

The CME group currently appears to have just a small share of its business in clearing OTC derivatives, relative to regulated futures.[41] The CME ClearPort began clearing interest rate swaps on October 18, 2010.[42] As of February 8, 2011, it had more than $900 million in outstanding notional interest rate swap contracts.[43] This is a fraction of a percent of the global interest rate swaps market.[44] CME ClearPort's buy-side participants are BlackRock, Citadel, Fannie Mae, Freddie Mac, and PIMCO. The sell-side participants are BofA Merrill Lynch, Barclays Capital, Citi, Credit Suisse, Deutsche Bank, Goldman Sachs, J.P. Morgan, Morgan Stanley, Nomura, and UBS.

CME ClearPort was originally created in May of 2002 to clear OTC natural gas products for CME. CME has also provided clearing services for credit default swap (CDS) contracts since 2009, but CME's CDS clearing business remains relatively small compared with ICE's.[45] News media also reported that ICE tends to clear the majority of CDS products that are cleared, whereas CME only clears a small amount.[46] By the end of 2009, ICE Trust had cleared more than $4 trillion worth of notional CDS contracts.[47] This represented 16% of the global CDS market. As of February 8, 2011, CME's net notional outstanding U.S. contracts equaled $33 million,[48] which represented a very small amount of the CDS market.[49]

CME Group's ownership structure is comparatively heterogeneous: 0.86% is owned by individual stakeholders; 29.67% is owned by mutual fund holders; and 37.78% is owned by other institutions.[50] The largest percentages of shares are owned by BackRock Fund Advisors (at 4.35%), Vanguard Group, Inc (at 3.61%), State Street Global Advisors (at 3.50%), Alliace Bernstein LP (at 3.30%), and Goldman Sachs Asset Management LP (at 2.81%).

ICE, like CME, has vertically integrated execution, clearing, and settling facilities. ICE is owned 0.28% by individuals, 31.41% by funds, and 70.10% by institutions.[51] Its largest shareholders are T. Rowe Price (at 9.82%), Sands Capital Management (at 5.64%), Delaware Management Business Trust (at 4.84%), and Vanguard Group (at 4.46%).[52] ICE has been clearing CDSs since 2009, when 10 major banks put forth funds to establish its OTC clearinghouse.[53] Along with LCH, it is the largest clearer of OTC derivatives, but mostly for the CDS market.

For the OTC market as a whole, the interest rate swaps market is by far the largest OTC product traded, representing about 93% of the notional amount of OTC derivatives.[54] LCH is the largest interest rate swap clearinghouse. LCH currently clears more than 40% of the interest rate swaps market. According to its 2009 annual report, LCH has more than $200 trillion outstanding in interest rate swap trades that it has cleared using its subsidiary, SwapClear.[55] This represents 57% of the global interest rate swaps market.[56]

Unlike CME, LCH's ownership is more concentrated. It is a holding company that was created as part of a merger in December 2003 to oversee LCH.Clearnet Limited and LCH.Clearnet SA.[57] 84% of its shares are owned by its users and 17% are owned by exchanges.[58] In 1980, long before LCH merged with Clearnet SA in 2003, its ownership was passed to a consortium of Britain's six largest banks. Its current board of directors includes members from Morgan Stanley, Goldman Sachs, the London Stock Exchange, ABN AMRO Bank N.V., Citigroup, HSBC, JP Morgan, Deutsche Bank, Barclays, and BNP Paribas—which are some of the leading OTC derivatives dealers.[59] LCH's corporate governance rules require that some of its key stakeholders be represented on the board of directors.[60] It also states that "shareholders have a particularly direct involvement in the business of the company and the group."[61]

On November 6, 2010, LCH.Clearnet Group Ltd., Europe's largest clearinghouse, completed a buyout of shareholders, boosting its largest users' stakes ending a nine-month struggle for control. LCH.Clearnet defines its biggest users as those contributing more than 1% of its total clearing fees. Its biggest users now own 63% of shares compared with 37% prior to the buyout.[62]

Adjustments to DCO ownership and governance structures may occur as a result of Dodd-Frank and CFTC and SEC rules. Many banks and clearinghouses are making moves to capitalize on the new push toward derivatives clearing.[63] To give some examples, Royal Bank of Scotland (RBS) joined CME's OTC clearing division in November 2010 and Wells Fargo Securities became a member in February 2011. LCH.Clearnet is due to launch a "buyside" service for interest rate swaps.[64]

Trends in Clearing and Trading

As mentioned above, over the past 10 years, there has been a trend toward vertical integration in the exchange and clearinghouse industry, amongst exchanges that trade OTC derivatives. Vertical integration is when an exchange that executes transactions in securities or derivatives joins together with an existing clearinghouse or makes moves to create a clearing division of its own to clear and settle all of its transactions. Examples of such integration include CME Group (in 2006),[65] LCH.CLearnet (early 2000s), and ICE (mid- to late 2000s).[66]

CME Group is the product of a merger between the Chicago Mercantile Exchange (CME) and the Chicago Board of Trade (CBOT) that occurred in 2006. The merger occurred after the Board of Trade Clearing Corporation (BTCC) agreed to clear Eurex transactions.[67] Eurex's entrance into the market directly competed with CBOT. In response, CBOT rescinded its rule that required its members to clear through the Board of Trade Clearing Corporation (BTCC), and required them to clear through CME instead. In 2006, the two were finally merged.

ICE Clear US was originally the New York Cotton Exchange Clearing Association from 1915. It later became the Commodity Clearing Corporation.[68] To expand its futures business it merged with the International Petroleum Exchange (IPE), which later became ICE Futures Europe.[69] It then partnered with the Chicago Climate Exchange (CCX) in 2005, to host its OTC emissions markets; and merged with the New York Board of Trade (NYBOT) in January 2007.[70]

Why have exchanges become vertically integrated with clearinghouses? Some academics argue that integration of trade, execution, and settlement in an exchange improves the efficiency of the exchange because it economizes its transaction costs.[71] This happens because the merged entity then has the option of denying other entities access to its clearing and settlement services—particularly those entities which trade products that are already traded on the integrated exchange. Vertical integration can also be beneficial because it allows the exchange to organize its transactions in a way that eliminates double marginalization (because it would clear and settle through its own facilities) and would help to avoid holdups. Vertical integration has been a component of financial markets long before exchanges and clearinghouses started working on OTC transactions. The Chicago Board of Options Exchange, for example, formed its central counterparty clearinghouses in 1973.[72]

There is also a trend toward horizontal integration, whereby exchanges merge to compete with other exchange entities over derivatives, futures, and options trading. For example, in February, 2011 news media reported that the New York Stock Exchange (NYSE) was nearing an agreement to be taken over by Deutsche Borse AG.[73] Such a merger would create the world's largest financial exchange.[74] The takeover would be the latest in a decade of mergers by exchanges around the world looking for new sources of growth, and competing with smaller rivals that have been quicker to embrace new and lucrative kinds of trading.[75] Competition has also been growing from electronic exchanges, and those trading derivative contracts such as options and futures. For instance, a rising competitor for NYSE and Deutsche Borse AG is CME Group Inc.[76] The *Wall Street Journal* predicted that such a new entity would supplant CME Group as the world's largest futures exchange and create the biggest U.S. options group, as measured by contract volume.

ACKNOWLEDGMENTS

Teisha Ruggiero, former CRS Fellow, co-authored the original version of this report. The author would also like to acknowledge valuable help in preparing this report from CRS Specialist Mark Jickling, CRS Analyst Christopher M. Davis, and former CRS Fellow Donna Nordenberg.

End Notes

[1] For an overview of Dodd-Frank's derivatives provisions, see CRS Report R41398, *The Dodd-Frank Wall Street Reform and Consumer Protection Act: Title VII, Derivatives*, by Mark Jickling and Kathleen Ann Ruane.

[2] A clearinghouse generally accepts only contracts brought to it by a member firm. Non-member brokers must establish a correspondent relationship with a member in order to clear their customers' transactions.

[3] Systemic risk is risk that can potentially cause instability for large parts of the financial system. For more on systemic risk, see CRS Report R41384, *The Dodd-Frank Wall Street Reform and Consumer Protection Act: Systemic Risk and the Federal Reserve*, by Marc Labonte.

[4] See CRS Report R40438, Federal Government Assistance for American International Group (AIG), by Baird Webel.

[5] For the mechanics of derivatives, see CRS Report R40646, *Derivatives Regulation in the 111th Congress*, by Mark Jickling and Rena S. Miller.

[6] Also referred to as a central counterparty or as a derivatives clearing organization (DCO).

[7] See CRS Report R41384, The Dodd-Frank Wall Street Reform and Consumer Protection Act: Systemic Risk and the Federal Reserve, by Marc Labonte.

[8] Section 723 deals with swaps under CFTC regulation, while section 763 sets out parallel requirements for security-based swaps, regulated by the SEC.

[9] The SEC and CFTC clearing rules are due to be in place by July 21, 2011, one year from enactment.

[10] Regulators may, however, designate classes of swaps that should be cleared, even if no DCO is clearing them. If such swaps are still not cleared, the regulators may impose conditions on transactions in them. Regulators may also write rules to prevent evasion of the clearing mandate.

[11] SEC, "Ownership Limitations and Governance Requirements for Security-Based Swap Clearing Agencies, Security-Based Swap Execution Facilities, and National Securities

Exchanges With Respect to Security-Based Swaps Under Regulation MC; Proposed Rule," *Federal Register*, vol. 75, October 26, 2010, p. 65885.

[12] CFTC, "Requirements for Derivatives Clearing Organizations, Designated Contract Markets, and Swap Execution Facilities Regarding the Mitigation of Conflicts of Interest," *Federal Register*, vol. 75, October 18, 2010, p. 63732.

[13] For text of amendment, see U.S. Congress, House, Committee on Rules, *Report to Accompany H.Res. 964*, H. Rept, 111-370, 111th Cong., 1st sess. (Washington: GPO, 2009), pp. 188-192.

[14] "House-Senate Conference Committee Holds A Meeting on Walls Street Reform and Consumer Protection Act." *Financial Markets Regulatory Wire*, June 24, 2010, CQ Transcriptions, LLC.

[15] Ibid.

[16] Ibid.

[17] Ibid.

[18] *Congressional Record*, daily edition, vol. 156, June 30, 2010, p. H5217.

[19] CFTC, "Requirements for Derivatives Clearing Organizations, Designated Contract Markets, and Swap Execution Facilities Regarding the Mitigation of Conflicts of Interest," *Federal Register*, vol. 75, October 18, 2010, p. 63732.

[20] CFTC, "Governance Requirements for Derivatives Clearing Organizations, Designated Contract Markets, and Swap Execution Facilities; Additional Requirements Regarding the Mitigation of Conflicts of Interest," *Federal Register*, vol. 76, January 6, 2011, p. 722.

[21] SEC, "17 CFR Part 242: Ownership Limitations and Governance Requirements for Security-Based Swap Clearing Agencies, Security-Based Swap Execution Facilities, and National Securities Exchanges With Respect to Security-Based Swaps Under Regulation MC," *Federal Register*, vol. 75, October. 26, 2010, p. 65882.

[22] The SEC rule does the same thing, but refers to these as "specified entities."

[23] The ownership limits will also apply to designated contract markets (futures exchanges) and swap execution facilities (created by Dodd-Frank).

[24] Section 726(a) of the Dodd-Frank Act; 15 U.S.C. § 8323(a).

[25] See, e.g., Comment No. 26325, Comment for Proposed Rule 75 FR 63732, from Ernest C. Goodrich Jr. for Deutsche Bank AG, October 26, 2010, at http://comments.cftc.gov/PublicComments/ViewComment.aspx?id=26325&SearchText=. See also Comment No. 26411, Comment for Proposed Rule 75 FR 63732, from Robert Pickel for the International Swaps and Derivatives Association, Inc., November 16, 2010, at http://comments.cftc.gov/ PublicComments/ViewComment.aspx?id=26411&SearchText=. Also see Comment for File No. S7-27-10, from John S. Willian for Goldman, Sachs & Co., November 18, 2010, at http://www.sec.gov/comments/s7-27-10/s72710.shtml. See also Comment No. 26410, Comment for Proposed Rule 75 FR 63732, from Janet McGinness for NYSE Liffe US LLC, November 16, 2010, at http://comments.cftc.gov/PublicComments/ViewComment.aspx?id=26410&SearchText=.

[26] Ibid., p. 63753. The European Commission announced its proposal on September 15, 2010. See European Commission, "Proposal for a regulation of the European Parliament and of the Council on OTC derivatives, central counterparties and trade repositories," at http://eur-lex.europa.eu/LexUriServ/LexUriServ.do?uri= CELEX:52010PC0484:EN:NOT.

[27] CFTC, "Conflicts of Interest in Self-Regulation and Self-Regulatory Organizations ("SROs")," *Federal Register,* vol. 72, February 14, 2007, p. 6936. (Hereinafter cited as *2007 DCM Conflicts Release.*)

[28] Section 735(b) of the Dodd-Frank Act; 7 U.S.C. § 7(d)(16).

[29] *2007 DCM Conflicts Release*, p. 6937. The acceptable practices, among other things, require 35% representation of public directors on a DCM board and set rules requiring oversight committees, but do not establish ownership limits.

[30] Ibid, p. 6939. The CFTC also expresses concern that sustained competition between DCMs and SEFs for the same swaps contracts may exacerbate certain structural conflicts of interest.

[31] Section 725(c) of the Dodd-Frank Act; 7 U.S.C. § 7a-1(c)(2).

[32] No director may qualify as an independent director unless the full board affirmatively determines that the director does not have a material relationship with (1) the DCO or an affiliate, or (2) a DCO member or affiliate.

[33] See, e.g., Comment No. 27266, Comment for Proposed Rule 75 FR 63732, from Kathleen M. Cronin for CME Group Inc. November, 17 2010, at http://comments.cftc.gov/PublicComments/ViewComment.aspx?id=27266& SearchText=. See also e.g., Comment No. 26474, Comment for Proposed Rule 75 FR 63732, from James B. Fuqua for UBS Securities LLC. November 17, 2010, at http://comments.cftc.gov/PublicComments/ViewComment.aspx?id= 26474&SearchText=. See also e.g., Comment No. 26422, Comment for Proposed Rule 75 FR 63732, from Timothy G. McDermott for Nadex, November 17, 2010, at http://comments.cftc.gov/PublicComments/ViewComment.aspx?id= 26422&SearchText=

[34] See, e.g., Comment No. 26429, Comment for Proposed Rule 75 FR 63732, from Thomas Book for Eurex Clearing AG. November 17, 2010, at http://comments.cftc.gov/PublicComments/ViewComment.aspx?id=26429&SearchText=. See also Comment No. 26474, Comment for Proposed Rule 75 FR 63732, from James B. Fuqua for UBS Securities LLC. November 17, 2010, at http://comments.cftc.gov/PublicComments/ViewComment.aspx?id=26474&SearchText=.

[35] See, e.g., Comment No. 26700, Comment for Proposed Rule 75 FR 63732, from Edward J. Rosen for Bank of America Merrill Lynch; Barclays Capital; BNP Paribas; Citi; Credit Agricole Corporate and Investment Bank; Credit Suisse Securities (USA); Deutsche Bank AG; HSBC; Morgan Stanley; Nomura Securities International, Inc.; PNC Bank, National Association; UBS Securities LLC; Wells Fargo & Company. Please see attachment. December 3, 2010, at http://comments.cftc.gov/PublicComments/ViewComment.aspx?id=26700&SearchText=.

[36] See, e.g., Comment No. 26700, Comment for Proposed Rule 75 FR 63732, from Edward J. Rosen for Bank of America Merrill Lynch; Barclays Capital; BNP Paribas; Citi; Credit Agricole Corporate and Investment Bank; Credit Suisse Securities (USA); Deutsche Bank AG; HSBC; Morgan Stanley; Nomura Securities International, Inc.; PNC Bank, National Association; UBS Securities LLC; Wells Fargo & Company. Please see attachment. December 3, 2010, at http://comments.cftc.gov/PublicComments/ViewComment.aspx?id=26700&SearchText=.

[37] See, e.g., Comment No. 26410, Comment for Proposed Rule 75 FR 63732, from Janet McGinness for NYSE Liffe US LLC. November 16, 2010, at http://comments.cftc.gov/PublicComments/ViewComment.aspx?id=26410&SearchText=

[38] See, e.g., Comment No. 26486, Comment for Proposed Rule 75 FR 63732, from Sherrod Brown for United States Senate. November 18, 2010, at http://comments.cftc.gov/PublicComments/ViewComment.aspx?id=26486& SearchText=.

[39] See, e.g., Comment No. 26291, Comment for Proposed Rule 75 FR 63732, from Stephen F. Lynch for U.S. House of Representatives. October 18, 2010, at http://comments.cftc.gov/PublicComments/ViewComment.aspx?id=26291& SearchText=. See also Comment No. 26341, Comment for Proposed Rule 75 FR 63732, from Michael E.

Conflicts of Interest in Derivatives Clearing 95

Capuano for U.S. House of Representatives, October 29, 2010, at http://comments.cftc.gov/PublicComments/ViewComment.aspx? id=26341&SearchText=. See also Comment No. 26975, Comment for Proposed Rule 75 FR 63732, from Michael N. Castle for U.S. House of Representatives, November 14, 2010, at http://comments.cftc.gov/PublicComments/ ViewComment.aspx?id=26975&SearchText=. See also Comment No. 26432, Comment for Proposed Rule 75 FR 63732, from Joshua Miller for Senate Corporations Committee, November 17, 2010, at http://comments.cftc.gov/PublicComments/ViewComment.aspx?id=26432&SearchText=

[40] LCH.Clearnet appears to be an exception to this trend. See Craig Pirrong, "The Industrial Organization of Execution, Clearing and Settlement in Financial Markets," December 21, 2006.

[41] The CME's main clearing business right now is interest rate futures; see p. 21 of CME 10-Q form for the SEC for 2010, at http://www.sec.gov/Archives/edgar/data/1156375/000119312510250139/d10q.htm. It operates four exchanges: The Chicago Mercantile Exchange (CME), The Board of Trade of the City of Chicago (CBOT), The New York Mercantile Exchange (NYMEX), and the Commodity Exchange (COMEX). It operates its clearing business through CME ClearPort. For its plans to capture more of the European OTC market, see "CME Group Reports Fourth Quarter Earnings and Plans for Returning More Capital to Shareholders," by Michael Wong for Morning Star, February 3, 2011, at http://torontostar.morningstar.ca/globalhome/industry

[42] See CME Group, "CME Group Begins Clearing OTC Interest Rate Swaps," press release, October 18, 2010, http://cmegroup.mediaroom.com/index.php?item=3073&pagetemplate=article&s=43.

[43] CME Group, "Interest Rate Swaps Market Data Reports," press release, February 2, 2011, http://www.cmegroup.com/trading/interest-rates/cleared-otc/irs.html.

[44] The BIS estimates that in 2010 interest rate swaps totaled $347 trillion. See Bank of International Settlements, *Amounts outstanding of over-the-counter (OTC) derivatives*, http://www.bis.org/statistics

[45] See Christine Birkner, "Credit default swaps clearing buy side access achieved," *Futuresmag.com*, February 1, 2010, at http://www.futuresmag.com/Issues/2010/February-2010/Pages/Credit-default-swaps-buy-side-access

[46] Ibid.

[47] From January to September in 2010, Ice Trust, ICE's U.S. clearinghouse, cleared $4.1 trillion of CDS notional value. See p. 27 of Securities Exchange Commission, "Intercontinental Exchange Form 10-Q," press release, September 10, 2010, http://www.sec.gov/Archives/edgar/data/1174746/000119312510241968/d10q.htm.

[48] See chart for CME Group, CDS Market Data Reports, at http://www.cmegroup.com/trading/cds/cds-data.html.

[49] DTCC estimates the net notional amount of the CDS market to be $2.3 trillion as of December 31, 2010, while the gross notional reported was $25.5 trillion. See ISDA, CDS Marketplace, at http://www.isdacdsmarketplace.com/ market_statistics.

[50] CNNMoney, "CME Group Inc," press release, 2010, http://money.cnn.com/quote/shareholders

[51] Morningstar, "CME Group Inc.," press release, January 31, 2011, http://investors shareholders-overview.html?t=CME.

[52] Ibid.

[53] In 2009, Bank of America, Barclays Capital, Citigroup, Credit Suisse, Deutsche Bank, Goldman Sachs, J.P. Morgan, Merrill Lynch, Morgan Stanley, and UBS became the initial clearing members of ICE Trust. Each contributed "significantly" to the trust's guarantee fund. See ICE, press release, 2009. http://ir.theice.com/releasedetail.cfm?ReleaseID=369373. This was during ICE's March 6, 2009, acquisition of The Clearing Corporation (TCC)—which cleared U.S. futures and OTC emissions.

[54] According to ISDA's mid-year 2010 survey, the total notional amount outstanding for OTC derivatives was around $466.8 trillion, of which interest rate derivatives (swaps, options, cross-currency) comprised $434.1 trillion (around 93%). Credit derivatives, on the other hand, made up $26.3 trillion (this included credit default swaps, single name indexes, etc.). See ISDA, press release, 2010, http://www.isda.org/media

[55] LCH.Clearnet, "2009 Annual Report and Consolidated Financial Statement," press release, 2009, http://www.lchclearnet.com/Images/2009%20Annual%20Report%20and%20Consolidated%20Financial%20Statements_tcm6-53486.pdf.

[56] The BIS estimated the notional amount of interest rate swaps outstanding in 2009 to be $349 trillion. See http://www.bis.org/statistics

[57] LCH.Clearnet, "2009 Annual Report and Consolidated Financial Statement," press release, 2009, http://www.lchclearnet.com/Images/2009%20Annual%20Report%20and%20Consolidated%20Financial%20Statements_tcm6-53486.pdf.

[58] Ibid.

[59] For information on LCH's ownership structure see LCH.Clearnet, "2009 Annual Report and Consolidated Financial Statement," press release, 2009, http://www.lchclearnet.com/Images/2009%20Annual%20Report%20and%20Consolidated%20Financial%20Statements_tcm6-53486.pdf. For information on OTC derivatives trading, see ISDA, "News Release," press release, October 25, 2010, http://www.isda.org/media press/2010/press102510.html. Note that the ISDA release says: "The five largest US-based dealers reported a notional amount outstanding of $172.3 trillion, which is 37 percent of the total amount. This contrasts with other reports in which the five largest US-based dealers appear to hold 95 percent of outstandings and dominate the OTC derivatives market. The difference lies in the fact that the ISDA Survey takes into account the global scope and scale of the derivatives business, while the other figures compare the five largest U.S.-based dealers to the total held only by U.S. bank holding companies."

[60] See p. 82 of LCH.Clearnet, "LCH Annual Report," press release, 2009, http://www.lchclearnet.com/Images/2009%20Annual%20Report%20and%20Consolidated%20Financial%20Statements_tcm6-53486.pdf.

[61] Ibid.

[62] Lisa Brennan, "Mounting Conflicts at Exchanges, Clearinghouses Prompt Concern," *Bloomberg*, January 20, 2010, available at http://www.bloomberg.com/apps/news?pid=newsarchive&sid=ayyhPhL2Vz2c.

[63] See Jeremy Grant, "Wells Fargo becomes clearing member of CME," *Financial Times*, February 1, 2011. Also see Louise Story, "A Secretive Banking Elite Rules Trading on Derivatives," *New York Times*, December 10, 2010.

[64] Ibid.

[65] Craig Pirrong, "The Industrial Organization of Execution, Clearing and Settlement in Financial Markets," *Bauer College of Business, University of Houston*, December 21, 2006, in appendix.
[66] See Intercontinental Exchange, "A History of Transparent Markets," press release, February 10, 2011, https://www.theice.com/history
[67] Craig Pirrong, "The Industrial Organization of Execution, Clearing and Settlement in Financial Markets," *Bauer College of Business, University of Houston*, December 21, 2006, in appendix.
[68] See Intercontinental Exchange, "A History of Transparent Markets," press release, February 10, 2011, https://www.theice.com/history
[69] Ibid.
[70] Ibid.
[71] Craig Pirrong, "The Industrial Organization of Execution, Clearing and Settlement in Financial Markets," *Bauer College of Business, University of Houston*, December 21, 2006, p.1.
[72] Ibid.
[73] E.S. Browning, Jacob Bunge, and Aaron Lucchetti, "Germans in Talks to Buy Big Board," *The Wall Street Journal*, February 10, 2011.
[74] Ibid. Note, Deutsche Borse owns 50% of Eurex Clearing, AG which clears all Deutsche Borse tock trades. See Craig Pirrong, "The Industrial Organization of Execution, Clearing and Settlement in Financial Markets," *Bauer College of Business, University of Houston*, December 21, 2006, p.1.
[75] Ibid.
[76] Ibid.

In: Derivatives Reform and Regulation	ISBN: 978-1-61324-935-2
Editor: Aidan B. Lynch	© 2011 Nova Science Publishers, Inc.

Chapter 4

THE DODD-FRANK WALL STREET REFORM AND CONSUMER PROTECTION ACT: TITLE VII, DERIVATIVES[*]

Mark Jickling and Kathleen Ann Ruane

SUMMARY

The financial crisis implicated the unregulated over-the-counter (OTC) derivatives market as a major source of systemic risk. A number of firms used derivatives to construct highly leveraged speculative positions, which generated enormous losses that threatened to bankrupt not only the firms themselves but also their creditors and trading partners. Hundreds of billions of dollars in government credit were needed to prevent such losses from cascading throughout the system. AIG was the best-known example, but by no means the only one.

Equally troublesome was the fact that the OTC market depended on the financial stability of a dozen or so major dealers. Failure of a dealer would have resulted in the nullification of trillions of dollars worth of contracts and would have exposed derivatives counterparties to sudden risk and loss, exacerbating the cycle of deleveraging and withholding of credit that characterized the crisis. During the crisis, all the major dealers came under stress, and even though derivatives dealing was not generally the direct source of financial weakness, a collapse of the $600 trillion

---

[*] This is an edited, reformatted and augmented version of a Congressional Research Service publication, CRS Report for Congress R41398, from www.crs.gov, dated August 30, 2010.

OTC derivatives market was imminent absent federal intervention. The first group of Troubled Asset Relief Program (TARP) recipients included nearly all the large derivatives dealers.

The Dodd-Frank Act (P.L. 111-203) sought to remake the OTC market in the image of the regulated futures exchanges. Crucial reforms include a requirement that swap contracts be cleared through a central counterparty regulated by one or more federal agencies. Clearinghouses require traders to put down cash (called initial margin) at the time they open a contract to cover potential losses, and require subsequent deposits (called maintenance margin) to cover actual losses to the position. The intended effect of margin requirements is to eliminate the possibility that any firm can build up an uncapitalized exposure so large that default would have systemic consequences (again, the AIG situation). The size of a cleared position is limited by the firm's ability to post capital to cover its losses. That capital protects its trading partners and the system as a whole.

Swap dealers and major swap participants—firms with substantial derivatives positions—will be subject to margin and capital requirements above and beyond what the clearinghouses mandate. Swaps that are cleared will also be subject to trading on an exchange, or an exchange-like "swap execution facility," regulated by either the Commodity Futures Trading Commission (CFTC) or the Securities and Exchange Commission (SEC), in the case of security-based swaps. All trades will be reported to data repositories, so that regulators will have complete information about all derivatives positions. Data on swap prices and trading volumes will be made public.

The new law provides exceptions to the clearing and trading requirements for commercial end-users, or firms that use derivatives to hedge the risks of their nonfinancial business operations. Regulators may also provide exemptions for smaller financial institutions. Even trades that are exempt from the clearing and exchange-trading requirements, however, will have to be reported to data repositories or directly to regulators.

This report describes some of the new requirements placed on the derivatives market by the Dodd-Frank Act. It will not be updated.

INTRODUCTION

Prior to the financial crisis that began in 2007, over-the-counter (OTC) derivatives were generally regarded as a beneficial financial innovation that distributed financial risk more efficiently and made the financial system more stable, resilient, and resistant to shocks. The crisis essentially reversed this view. The Dodd-Frank Act (P.L. 111-203) attempts to address the aspect of the OTC market that appeared most troublesome in the crisis: the market permitted enormous exposure to risk to grow out of the sight of regulators and other traders. Derivatives exposures that could not be readily quantified exacerbated panic and uncertainty about the true financial condition of other market participants, contributing to the freezing of credit markets. Under Dodd-Frank, risk exposures of major financial institutions must be backed by capital, minimizing the shock to the financial system should such a firm fail. In addition, regulators will have information about the size and distribution of possible losses during periods of market volatility.

Background

Derivative contracts are an array of financial instruments with one feature in common: their value is linked to changes in some underlying variable, such as the price of a physical commodity, a stock index, or an interest rate. Derivatives contracts—futures contracts, options, and swaps[1]— gain or lose value as the underlying rates or prices change, even though the holder may not actually own the underlying asset.

Thousands of firms use derivatives to manage risk. For example, a firm can protect itself against increases in the price of a commodity that it uses in production by entering into a derivative contract that will gain value if the price of the commodity rises. A notable instance of this type of hedging strategy was Southwest Airlines' derivatives position that allowed it to buy jet fuel at a low fixed price in 2008 when energy prices reached record highs. When used to hedge risk, derivatives can protect businesses (and sometimes their customers as well) from unfavorable price shocks.

Others use derivatives to seek profits by betting on which way prices will move. Such speculators provide liquidity to the market—they assume the risks that hedgers wish to avoid. The combined trading activity of hedgers and speculators provides another public benefit: price discovery. By incorporating all known information and expectations about future prices, derivatives markets generate prices that often serve as a reference point for transactions in the underlying cash markets.

Although derivatives trading had its origins in agriculture, today most derivatives are linked to financial variables, such as interest rates, foreign exchange, stock prices and indices, and the creditworthiness of issuers of bonds. The market is measured in the hundreds of trillions of dollars, and billions of contracts are traded annually.

Derivatives have also played a part in the development of complex financial instruments, such as bonds backed by pools of other assets. They can be used to create "synthetic" securities—contracts structured to replicate the returns on individual securities or portfolios of stocks, bonds, or other derivatives. Although the basic concepts of derivative finance are neither new nor particularly difficult, much of the most sophisticated financial engineering of the past few decades has involved the construction of increasingly complex mathematical models of how markets move and how different financial variables interact. Derivatives trading is often a primary path through which such research reaches the marketplace.

Since 2000, growth in derivatives markets has been explosive (although the financial crisis has caused some retrenchment since 2008). Between 2000 and the end of 2008, the volume of derivatives contracts traded on exchanges,[2] such as futures exchanges, and the notional value of total contracts traded in the over-the-counter (OTC) market[3] grew by 475% and 522%, respectively. By contrast, during the credit and housing booms that occurred over the same period, the value of corporate bonds and home mortgage debt outstanding grew by only 95% and 115%, respectively.[4]

Pre-Dodd-Frank Act Market Structure and Regulation

The various types of derivatives are used for the same purposes—avoiding business risk, or hedging, and taking on risk in search of speculative profits. Prior to the Dodd-Frank Act, however, the instruments were traded on different types of markets. Futures contracts are traded on exchanges regulated by the Commodity Futures Trading Commission (CFTC); stock options on exchanges under the Securities and Exchange Commission (SEC); and all swaps (and security-based swaps, as well as some options) were traded OTC, and were not regulated by anyone.

Exchanges are centralized markets where all the buying and selling interest comes together. Traders who want to buy (or take a long position) interact with those who want to sell (or go short), and deals are made and prices reported throughout the day. In the OTC market, contracts are made bilaterally, typically between a dealer and an end user, and there was generally no requirement that the price, the terms, or even the existence of the contract be disclosed to a regulator or to the public.

Derivatives can be volatile contracts, and the normal expectation is that there will be big gains and losses among traders. As a result, there is an issue of market integrity. How do the longs know that the shorts will be able to meet their obligations, and vice versa? A market where billions of contracts change hands is impossible if all traders must investigate the creditworthiness of the other trader, or counterparty. The exchange market deals with this credit risk problem in one way, the OTC market in another way. How this risk—often called counterparty risk—must be managed was a key element of the reforms implemented by the Dodd-Frank Act.

Market Structure for Cleared and Exchange-Traded Derivatives

The exchanges deal with the issue of credit risk with a clearinghouse.[5] The process is shown in **Figure 1** below: (1) two traders agree on a transaction on the exchange floor or on an electronic platform. (2) Once the trade is made, it goes to the clearinghouse, which guarantees payment to both parties. (3) In effect, the original contract between long and short traders is now two contracts, one between each trader and the clearinghouse. Traders then do not have to worry about counterparty default because the clearinghouse stands behind all trades.

But the credit risk remains: how does the clearinghouse ensure that it can meet its obligations? Clearing depends on a system of margin, or collateral. Before the trade, both the long and short traders have to deposit an initial margin payment with the clearinghouse to cover potential losses. Then at the end of each trading day, all contracts are repriced, or "marked to market," and all those who have lost money (because prices moved against them) must post additional margin (called variation or maintenance margin) to cover those losses before the next trading session. This is known as a margin call: traders must make good on their losses immediately, or their broker may close out their positions when trading opens the next day. The effect of the margin system is that no one can build up a large paper loss that could damage the clearinghouse in case of default: it is certainly possible to lose large amounts of money trading on the futures exchanges, but only on a "pay as you go" basis.

Market Structure for OTC Derivatives

In the OTC market, as shown on the right side of Figure 1, the long and short traders do not interact directly. Instead of a centralized marketplace, there is a network of dealers who stand ready to take either long or short positions, and make money on spreads and fees. The dealer absorbs the credit risk of customer default, while the customer faces the risk of dealer default. In this kind of market, one would expect the dealers to be the most solid and creditworthy financial institutions, and in fact the OTC market that emerged was dominated by two or three dozen firms—very large institutions like JP Morgan Chase, Goldman Sachs, Citigroup, and their foreign counterparts. Before 2007, such firms were generally viewed as too well diversified or too well managed to fail; in 2008, their fallibility was well established, and the pertinent question now is whether the government would still consider them to be too big to fail. (Title II of Dodd-Frank seeks to ensure that it will not.[6])

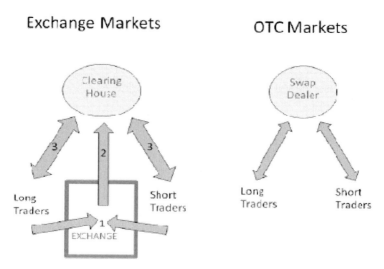

Source: CRS.

Figure 1. Pre-Dodd-Frank Act Derivatives Market Structures: Exchange and Over-the-Counter (OTC).

In the OTC market, some contracts required collateral or margin, but not all. There was no standard practice: all contract terms were negotiable. A trade group, the International Swaps and Derivatives Association (ISDA), published best practice standards for use of collateral, but compliance was voluntary.

Because there was no universal, mandatory system of margin, large uncollateralized losses could (and did) build up in the OTC market. Perhaps the best-known example in the crisis was AIG, which wrote about $1.8 trillion worth of credit default swaps guaranteeing payment if certain mortgage-backed securities defaulted or experienced other "credit events."[7] Many of AIG's contracts required it to post collateral as the credit quality of the underlying referenced securities (or AIG's own credit rating) deteriorated, but AIG did not post initial margin, as this was deemed unnecessary because of the firm's triple-A rating. As the subprime crisis worsened, AIG faced margin calls that it could not meet. To avert bankruptcy, with the risk of global financial chaos, the Federal Reserve and the Treasury put tens of billions of dollars into AIG, the bulk of which went to its derivatives counterparties.[8]

A key reform in Dodd-Frank is a mandate that many OTC swaps be cleared, which means that they will be subject to margin requirements. This will have the effect of combining features of the two market structures shown in Figure 1.

THE DODD-FRANK ACT'S CLEARING AND REPORTING REQUIREMENTS

In order to provide more stability to the OTC derivatives market, the Dodd-Frank Act requires that most derivatives contracts formerly traded exclusively in the OTC market be cleared and traded on exchanges. Thus, traders in these previously unregulated products will be required to post margin in the fashion described above and have their contracts repriced at the close of each trading day. This system likely will have the effect of regulating trade in these contracts more closely and providing greater transparency to the participants in the market and to the government regulators. Furthermore, the Dodd-Frank Act presumes that some derivatives contracts will still be traded in the OTC market; however, it grants regulators broader powers to obtain information about these derivatives and impose margin and capital requirements on them as well.

Clearing Requirement

Title VII of the Dodd-Frank Act creates largely parallel clearing and exchange trading requirements for swaps and security-based swaps as those terms are defined by Title VII and will be further defined by the CFTC and the SEC. Section 723 creates the clearing and exchange trading requirements for swaps over which the CFTC has jurisdiction.[9] Section 763 creates largely parallel requirements for security-based swaps over which the SEC has authority.[10]

If a swap or security-based swap is required to be cleared, the final version of the Dodd-Frank Act makes it unlawful for parties to enter into swaps or security-based swaps unless the transaction has been submitted for clearing.[11] There are two ways in which a swap or security-based swap may become subject to the clearing requirement.[12] In the first way, the agency of jurisdiction is required to engage in an ongoing review of the products it has jurisdiction over to determine whether a particular swap, security-based swap, group, or class of such contracts should be subject to the clearing requirement. In the House-passed version of the clearing requirement, determinations made by the agency in this manner would not have resulted in those transactions becoming subject to the clearing requirement, because in order to be subject to the clearing requirement, the agency had to make its determination pursuant to a submission of the transaction by a derivatives clearing organization or a clearing agency.[13] The Senate-passed version was more similar to the eventual statutory language in that determinations made by the agency of its own initiative regarding transactions required to be cleared may have been subject to the clearing requirement, without having to first be submitted to the agency as a transaction that a derivatives clearing organization or clearing agency intended to offer for clearing.[14] Determinations made on the initiative of the commissions will be discussed further in the "Prevention of Evasion" section below.

The second way in which a swap or security-based swap may become subject to the clearing requirement under the Dodd-Frank Act is upon submission to the CFTC or the SEC. When a derivatives clearing organization[15] (swaps) or clearing agency[16] (security-based swaps) decides to accept a swap or security-based swap for clearing, the act requires the organization to submit the transactions to the relevant commission for a determination as to whether the transactions should be required to be cleared. Furthermore, upon enactment of the Dodd-Frank Act, all swaps and security-based swaps that were listed for clearing by derivatives clearing organizations and clearing agencies at the time of passage were deemed submitted to the SEC and the CFTC for a determination of whether the clearing requirement should apply.

Following submission to the agencies, the agencies have 90 days to determine whether the swaps or security-based swaps are subject to the clearing requirement, unless the submitting organization agrees to an extension. When making that determination, the agencies must consider (1) "the existence of significant outstanding notional exposures, trading liquidity, and adequate pricing data"; (2) "the availability of rule framework, capacity, operational expertise and resources, and credit support infrastructure to clear the contract on terms consistent with material terms and trading conventions on which the contract is then traded"; (3) "the effect on the mitigation of systemic risk ... "; (4) "the effect on competition, including appropriate fees and charges ... "; and (5) "the existence of reasonable legal certainty in the event of the insolvency of the relevant derivatives clearing organization or 1 or more of its clearing members with regard to the treatment of customer and swap counterparty positions, funds, and property."[17] In the process of making these determinations, the agencies are also required to allow the public to comment on whether the clearing requirement should apply.

Should the CFTC or the SEC determine that a particular swap or security-based swap is required to be cleared, counterparties to that type of transaction may apply to stay the clearing requirement until the relevant agency "completes a review of the terms" of the swap or security-based swap and the clearing requirement.[18] Under the act, upon completing the review, the relevant agency may require the swap or security-based swap to be cleared, either unconditionally or subject to appropriate conditions. The relevant agency may also determine that the swap or security-based swap is not required to be cleared.

With certain exceptions, counterparties to swaps and security-based swaps that are required to be cleared must either execute the transactions on exchanges or specialized execution facilities.[19]

The Exchange-Trading Requirement

With certain exceptions, swaps and security-based swaps that are required to be cleared must also be executed on a regulated exchange or on a trading platform defined in the act as a swaps execution facility (SEF) or a security-based swaps execution facility (SBSEF). Such facilities must permit multiple market participants to trade by accepting bids or offers made by multiple participants in the facility.

The goal of the trading requirement is "to promote pre-trade price transparency in the swaps market."[20] Because the old OTC market was notably opaque, with complete price information available only to dealers, swaps customers were limited in their ability to shop for the best price or rate. The expectation is that as price information becomes more widely available, competition will produce narrower spreads and better prices.

SEFs and SBSEFs must comply with a number of core principles set out in the act. While these are somewhat less prescriptive than the regulation of exchanges where public customers are allowed to trade,[21] the new trading facilities have regulatory and administrative responsibilities far beyond what applied to OTC trading desks in the past. Among other things, SEFs and SBSEFs must

- establish and enforce rules to prevent trading abuses and to provide impartial access to the trading facility;
- ensure that swap contracts are not readily susceptible to manipulation;
- monitor trading to prevent manipulation, price distortion, and disruptions in the underlying cash market;
- set position limits;
- maintain adequate financial and managerial resources, including safeguards against operational risk;
- maintain an audit trail of all transactions;
- publish timely data on prices and trading volume;
- adopt emergency rules governing liquidation or transfer of trading positions as well as trading halts; and
- employ a chief compliance officer, who will submit an annual report to regulators.

During consideration of Dodd-Frank, a central issue of debate was the extent to which existing OTC derivatives trading platforms and mechanisms could be accommodated under the new regulatory regime. OTC trading practices ranged from individual telephone negotiations to electronic systems accessible to multiple participants. One concern was that if SEFs were too much like exchanges, the existing futures and securities exchanges would monopolize trading. On the other hand, if the SEF definition were too vague or general, the OTC market might remain opaque.

The bill reported by the Senate Banking Committee defined SEF as "an electronic trading system with pre-trade and post-trade transparency."[22] The explicit reference to "pre-trade" transparency does not appear in the final legislation, in part because of concerns that such a requirement was not compatible with the business models of a number of intermediaries, such as interdealer swap brokers providing anonymous execution services.[23]

As is the case with the clearing requirement, Dodd-Frank provides exceptions to the exchange-trading mandate. If no exchange or SEF or SBSEF makes a swap available for trading, the contract may be traded OTC. A swap that meets the end-user clearing exemption is likewise exempt from the trading requirement. We now discuss the end-user exemption.

End-User Exemption

Sections 723 and 763 of the Dodd-Frank Act provide exceptions to the clearing requirement for swaps and security-based swaps when one of the counterparties to the transaction is not a financial entity, is using the transaction to hedge or mitigate its own commercial risk, and notifies the relevant agency "how it generally meets its financial obligations associated with entering into non-cleared swaps."[24] This has been widely referred to as the end-user exemption because it applies only to transactions where at least one counterparty is "not a financial entity."[25] A financial entity for the purposes of this section is defined as a swap dealer, a security-based swap dealer, a major swap participant (MSP), a major security-based swap participant, a commodity pool, a private fund, an employee benefit plan, or a person predominantly engaged in activities that are in the business of banking, or in activities that are financial in nature.[26] Who is and who is not a financial entity is discussed further in the section describing MSPs.

The definition of who is eligible for the exception is more similar here to the House-passed version than to the Senate-passed version. However, one important change was made. The House-passed version allowed any parties who were not swap dealers or MSPs, who were using the transaction to hedge commercial risk, and who notified the relevant agency properly to qualify for the exemption.[27] The final version narrowed the availability of the exemption to parties who were not financial entities, as defined above, and the definition of financial entities arguably includes more parties than only those who are not dealers or MSPs. Furthermore, the definition of "financial entity" in the act appears to be more narrow than the definition of "financial entity" contained in the Senate-passed version, because the Senate bill's definition would have included "a person that is registered or required to be registered with the Commission."[28] Moreover, the act allows regulators to exclude depository institutions, farm credit institutions, and credit unions with $10 billion or less in assets from the definition of "financial entity." Thus, the final definition of end-users represented by the act appears to fall somewhere between the House and Senate definitions in the number of entities that may qualify.

The application of the clearing exemption provided by Sections 723 and 763 of the Dodd-Frank Act is at the discretion of the counterparty that qualifies for the exemption. Eligible counterparties may elect to clear the transaction, and may choose which derivatives clearing organization or clearing agency shall clear the transaction. Under the act, eligible counterparties may also use an affiliate ("including affiliate entities predominantly engaged in providing financing for the purchase of the merchandise or manufactured goods of the person") to engage in swaps or security-based swaps under the condition that the affiliate "act on behalf of the person [qualifying for the exemption] and as an agent, uses the swap to hedge or mitigate the commercial risk of the person or other affiliate of the person that is not a financial entity."[29] The CFTC and SEC may also prescribe rules to prevent abuse of this exception to the clearing requirement.

Prevention of Evasion

The CFTC and SEC are required by the Dodd-Frank Act to promulgate rules the commissions determined to be necessary to "prevent evasions of the mandatory clearing requirements under this Act." However, this rulemaking authority, while broad, carries additional nuance described below.

As noted above, the statutory scheme of Dodd-Frank creates two ways in which a swap or security-based swap may become subject to the clearing requirement. In one scenario, derivatives clearing organizations and clearing agencies submit the swaps and security-based swaps they intend to clear to the CFTC or SEC and the agency determines whether to apply the clearing requirement to the transactions. In the other scenario, the CFTC and SEC are required to engage in an ongoing independent review of swaps and security-based swaps under their jurisdiction to determine whether those transactions should be subject to the mandatory clearing requirement. It is thus possible that the CFTC and SEC could identify swaps and security-based swaps that "would otherwise be subject to the clearing requirement" but for the fact that no derivatives clearing organization or clearing agency accepts them for clearing.

In that event, the relevant agency (CFTC for swaps, and SEC for security-based swaps) is required to investigate the relevant facts and circumstances, issue a public report of its investigation, and "take such actions as the Commission determines to be necessary and in the public interest, which may include requiring the retaining of adequate margin or capital by parties to the swap [or security-based swap], group, category, type, or class of swaps [or security-based swaps]."[30] However, neither the CFTC nor the SEC may "adopt rules requiring a derivatives clearing organization [or clearing agency] to list for clearing a swap, group, category, type, or class of swaps if the clearing of the swap, group, category, type, or class of swaps would threaten the financial integrity of the derivatives organization."[31] Eliminated from the Dodd-Frank Act was a requirement in the Senate-passed version that the agencies exempt swaps and security-based swaps from the clearing and exchange trading requirements if no derivatives clearing organization or clearing agency accepts the transactions for clearing.[32] The removal of this proposed exemption from the act may grant the agencies more flexibility in determining how to treat transactions they identify for clearing, but that are not yet accepted for clearing by any derivatives clearing organization or clearing agency as the agencies begin to implement the clearing requirement of the Dodd-Frank Act.

Reporting of Swaps and Security-Based Swaps

Swaps must be reported to registered swap data repositories or the CFTC.[33] Security-based swaps must be reported to registered security-based swap data repositories or to the SEC.[34] The Dodd-Frank Act requires all swaps to be reported.[35] Swaps and security-based swaps entered into prior to the date of the enactment of Dodd-Frank Act are exempt from the clearing requirement if they are reported in accordance with the act. Swaps and security-based swaps entered into after the enactment of the Dodd-Frank Act, but prior to the imposition of the clearing requirement, are exempt from the clearing requirement if they are reported in accordance with the act.

Section 727 of Dodd-Frank outlines the public availability of swap transaction data.[36] The CFTC is required to promulgate rules regarding the public availability of such data. Swaps that are subject to the clearing requirement, and swaps that are not subject to the clearing requirement, but are nonetheless cleared at registered derivatives clearing organizations, must have real-time reporting for such transactions. Real-time reporting means to report data relating to a swap transaction, including price and volume, as soon as technologically practicable after the time at which the swap transaction has been executed. For swaps that are not cleared and are reported pursuant to subsection (h)(6) (requiring reporting prior to the implementation of the clearing requirement), real-time reporting is required in a manner that does not disclose the business transactions and market positions of any person. Lastly, for swaps that are determined to be required to be cleared under subsection (h)(2) (outlining the two ways, discussed above, in which swaps may become subject to the clearing requirement), but are not cleared, real-time public reporting is required as well. There is no parallel requirement in the act for security-based swaps, presumably because national securities exchanges upon which these transactions will be executed already provide comparable reporting.[37]

The act also creates reporting obligations for uncleared swaps and security-based swaps (including swaps and security-based swaps that qualify for the end-user exemption).[38] Swaps entered into prior to the enactment of the act will be subject to reporting and recordkeeping requirements for uncleared swaps and security-based swaps.[39] The purpose of these requirements, presumably, is to give the relevant commissions access to a more complete picture of the derivatives market, even for swaps that are not required to be cleared.

Major Swap Participant Definition

A basic theme in Dodd-Frank is that systemically important financial institutions should maintain capital cushions above and beyond what specific regulations require in order to compensate for the risk that their failure would pose to the financial system and the economy. In addition to the margin requirements that apply to individual derivatives contracts, major participants in derivatives markets will become subject to prudential regulation in Title VII. Two categories of regulated market participants are enumerated: swap dealers and major swap participants (together with the security-based swap equivalents).

Since the OTC dealer market is highly concentrated, the proposal that swap dealers be subject to additional prudential regulation was not controversial. Only a few dozen of the largest financial institutions will be affected. The question of how many firms should be included in the definition of major swap participant (MSP), however, was contentious. How many non-dealer and non-bank firms should become subject to prudential regulation?

Several MSP definitions were considered in the House; the version of H.R. 4173 that passed the House in December 2009 defined an MSP as a non-dealer holding a "substantial net position" in swaps, excluding positions held to hedge commercial risk, or whose counterparties would suffer "significant credit losses" in the event of an MSP default.[40] Neither "substantial net position," "significant loss," nor "commercial risk" was defined in the bill. However, the bill provided guidance to regulators: the first two terms were linked to "systemically important entities" that can "significantly impact the financial system through counterparty credit risk."

The MSP definition in the bill that passed the House in December 2009 sought to prevent regulators from defining the key terms ("substantial position," "significant loss," etc.) in a way that imposed prudential regulation on most firms that used derivatives to hedge risk. In addition, MSPs are required to clear their swap contracts, and the cost of clearing was regarded as burdensome for end-users. Under the House definition, it seemed plausible that relatively few firms would be defined as MSPs—Fannie Mae and Freddie Mac, a few large non-dealer banks and insurance companies, and perhaps a few large hedge funds.

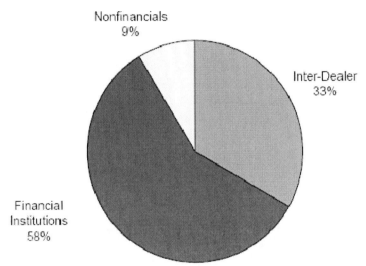

Source: Bank for International Settlements, *Regular OTC Derivatives Market Statistics*, May 2010.
Notes: Includes interest rate, foreign exchange, equity, and credit default swaps.

Figure 2. OTC Derivatives Contracts by Type of Counterparty, (Based on notional value of contracts as of December 2009).

There was an opposite concern: that if the end-user exemption were too broad, and the MSP definition too narrow, significant volumes of OTC trading might escape the new regulatory scheme. Figure 2 above suggests that if mandatory clearing were applied only to inter-dealer trades, two-thirds of the market would be unaffected. Nearly 60% of OTC contracts were between a dealer and another financial institution: how many of these would be covered?

While less than 10% of transactions involved nonfinancial counterparties, was it possible that risky trading activities could migrate from banks to nonfinancial firms if the exemption for hedging commercial risk were not in some way circumscribed?

Two versions of the MSP definition were considered in the Senate. The Banking Committee approved S. 3217 on April 15, 2010, including an MSP definition without the references to systemic importance that appeared in the House bill.[41] In other words, the regulators were given wide discretion to designate as MSPs firms that were not systemically important. The Senate Agriculture Committee produced another MSP definition, which was included in the bill that passed the Senate. It included "systemically significant" language generally similar to the House's, but added new prongs to the definition: an MSP would be any financial institution with a substantial position in any major swap category, or any financial entity that was highly leveraged.[42] This approach (together with changes to the clearing exemption limiting the exemption to nonfinancial entities) appeared likely to capture many swaps between dealers and other financial institutions, which make up more than half of the swap market.

Eliminating the clearing exemption for financial entities and bringing more financial firms under the MSP definition, as the Senate-passed bill did, had the virtue of bringing nearly all of the swaps trading under the new regulatory regime—the 33% of trades between dealers and the 58% between dealers and other financial institutions. This approach did raise questions of equity, that is, should a small community bank or credit union be subject to more stringent regulation than a giant nonfinancial corporation with a much greater volume of swaps outstanding?

The final version of the legislation made several changes to the MSP definition and the clearing requirement. The "highly leveraged" prong of the MSP definition was amended to clarify that it did not apply to regulated depository institutions, which are normally highly leveraged. In addition, as noted above, regulators were given discretion to exempt certain financial institutions with less than $10 billion in assets from the mandatory clearing requirement. The precise number of firms that are named MSPs (and the proportion of swaps that is ultimately cleared) depends on the SEC and CFTC rulemakings required by the act.

SECTION 716—PROHIBITION ON FEDERAL ASSISTANCE TO SWAPS ENTITIES

Section 716 originated in the Senate Agriculture Committee and was included in the bill that passed the Senate in May 2010. The section prohibited federal assistance, defined as the use of any funds to loan money to, buy the securities or other assets of, or to enter into "any assistance arrangement" with, a "swaps entity." Swaps entities included swap dealers and major swap participants (and the equivalents in security-based swaps), securities and futures exchanges, SEFs, and clearing organizations registered with the CFTC, the SEC, or any other federal or state agency.

The intent of the provision was to ensure that taxpayers would not have to bail out financial institutions engaged in risky derivatives trading. Such activity was deemed too risky to be under the federal safety net that covers insured depository institutions. Agriculture Committee Chairwoman Lincoln explained it this way:

> This provision seeks to ensure that banks get back to the business of banking. Under our current system, there are a handful of big banks that are simply no longer acting like banks.... In my view, banks were never intended to perform these [derivatives] activities, which have been the single largest factor to these institutions growing so large that taxpayers had no choice but to bail them out in order to prevent total economic ruin.[43]

Supporters of the original version of Section 716 described it as an appropriate means to compel banks to spin off their swap dealings, or to "push them out" into separately capitalized affiliates. Opponents of the measure argued that the definitions of federal assistance and swaps entity were so broadly drafted that there might be unanticipated consequences. For example, if Citigroup sold off its swap dealer operations, it would still have hundreds of billions of loans and other risky assets on its balance sheet, which it would need to hedge with interest rate swaps and other derivatives. This hedging activity would likely put the bank into the major swap participant category, and thus foreclose access to the discount window, FDIC insurance, and other features of the safety net. Similarly, if the Federal Reserve were supplying liquidity to the financial system during a future crisis, would it be prudent to deny such support to clearinghouses which represent concentrations of risk?

The conference committee adopted a modified version of Section 716, which narrowed the definitions of swaps entity and permitted banks to act as swap dealers under some circumstances. In the final legislation, exchanges, SEFs, and clearing organizations are not swaps entities. In addition, the term "swaps entity" does not include a major swap participant or major security-based swap participant that is an insured depository institution.

The final version clarifies that the prohibition on aid does not prevent a bank from creating an affiliate that is a swaps entity, provided that the affiliate complies with sections 23A and 23B of the Federal Reserve Act and other requirements of the Fed, the SEC, and the CFTC. Moreover, the bank itself may continue to act as a swaps dealer for contracts involving rates or reference assets that are permissible for investment by a national bank. This means that banks can continue as dealers in swaps linked to interest rates, currencies, government securities, and precious metals, but not other commodities or equities. Credit default swaps are treated as a special category: banks may deal in them if they are cleared by a derivatives clearing organization regulated by the SEC or CFTC. Dealing in uncleared credit default swaps, however, is not deemed to be a permissible bank activity.

Finally, Section 716 mandates that no taxpayer funds may be used to prevent the liquidation of a swaps entity. Any funds expended in such a liquidation proceeding, and not covered by the swaps entity's assets, may be recouped through assessments on the financial sector.

ENHANCED CFTC AUTHORITY OVER COMMODITIES MARKETS

In 2008, as energy and grain prices set new records, speculators in derivatives were blamed by some for price volatility and for price levels that many observers believed were not justified by the underlying economic fundamentals. Although the CFTC maintained that markets were functioning normally and that the price discovery process was not being distorted, the 110th Congress considered legislation intended to insulate commodity prices from the impact of excessive speculation and manipulation. Title VII includes a number of the specific provisions that appeared in those bills:

- **Margin.** The CFTC is given authority to set margin levels on the futures exchanges. (Previously, CFTC could change margins only in emergencies.) *Section 736.*
- **Position Limits.** The CFTC is directed to establish position limits for both swaps and futures. (CFTC has long had authority to set limits on the size of futures positions, but has generally delegated this function to the exchanges.) *Section 737.*
- **Anti-manipulation Authority.** New prohibitions against manipulation by means of false reporting or false information. *Section 753.*
- **Foreign Boards of Trade.** Foreign futures exchanges offering direct electronic access to their trading systems to U.S. persons must maintain rules regarding manipulation and excessive speculation comparable to those in U.S. law and regulation and must provide the CFTC with full market information.

Beyond these specific provisions, the increased transparency Dodd-Frank will bring to the OTC markets responds to a frequently heard criticism of the regulatory regime in 2008: that regulators could not be sure that price manipulation was not occurring because they lacked information about the volume of OTC trades and the identities of the big players in that market.

ACKNOWLEDGMENTS

Parts of the introductory material in this report are adapted from CRS Report R40965, *Key Issues in Derivatives Reform,* by Rena S. Miller.

End Notes

[1] For a description of the mechanics of these contracts, see CRS Report R40646, *Derivatives Regulation in the 111th Congress*, by Mark Jickling and Rena S. Miller.
[2] See Bank for International Settlements (BIS), Table 23B, for year 2000 turnover for derivative financial instruments traded on organized exchanges, available at http://www.bis.org/publ/qtrpdf/r_qa0206.pdf. For December 2008 figures for derivatives traded on organized exchanges, see BIS Quarterly Review, September 2009, International Banking and Financial Market Developments, available at http://www.bis.org/publ/qtrpdf/r_qt0909.pdf.

[3] See Bank for International Settlements (BIS), Statistical Annex, Table 19, December, 2000 figure for notional amount of total OTC contracts, available at http://www.bis.org/publ/qtrpdf/r_qa0206.pdf. See Bank for International Settlements (BIS), BIS Quarterly Review, September 2009, Statistical Annex, Table 19, for December 2008 figure for notional amount of total OTC contracts, available at http://www.bis.org/publ/qtrpdf/r_qa0909.pdf.

[4] Federal Reserve, *Flow of Funds Accounts of the United States*, September 17, 2009, accessible at http://www.federalreserve.gov/releases/z1/Current/z1r-1.pdf.

[5] Also referred to as a central counterparty or as a derivatives clearing organization (DCO).

[6] See CRS Report R41350, The Dodd-Frank Wall Street Reform and Consumer Protection Act: Issues and Summary, coordinated by Baird Webel.

[7] The credit events that trigger credit swap payments may include ratings downgrades, debt restructuring, late payment of interest or principal, as well as default.

[8] For an account of this process, see Office of the Special Inspector General for the Troubled Asset Relief Program ("SIGTARP"), *Factors Affecting Efforts to Limit Payments to AIG Counterparties*, November 17, 2009.

[9] Section 723 of the Dodd-Frank Act (to be codified at 7 U.S.C. §2).

[10] Section 763(a) of the Dodd-Frank Act (to be codified at 15 U.S.C. § 78a *et seq.*).

[11] Section 723(a)(3) of the Dodd-Frank Act (to be codified at 7 U.S.C. §2(h)(1)) (swaps); Section 763(a) of the Dodd-Frank Act (to be codified at 15 U.S.C. § 78a *et seq.*)(security-based swaps).

[12] Section 723(a)(3) of the Dodd-Frank Act (to be codified at 7 U.S.C. §2(h)(2)) (swaps); Section 763(a) of the Dodd-Frank Act (to be codified at 15 U.S.C. § 78a *et seq.*)(security-based swaps).

[13] Sections 3103 and 3203 of H.R. 4173 (as passed by the House).

[14] Sections 723(a) and 763 of H.R. 4173 (as passed by the Senate).

[15] Rules for the registration and regulation of derivatives clearing organizations are enacted by Section 725 of the Dodd-Frank Act (to be codified at 7 U.S.C. §7a-1).

[16] Rules for the registration and regulation of clearing agencies were enacted by Section 763(b) of the Dodd-Frank Act (to be codified at 15 U.S.C. §78a-1).

[17] Section 723(a)(3) of the Dodd-Frank Act (to be codified at 7 U.S.C. §2(h)) (swaps); Section 763(a) of the Dodd-Frank Act (to be codified at 15 U.S.C. § 78a *et seq.*)(security-based swaps). Similar considerations were mandated by the Senate passed version of the bill, but those considerations were to be applied to the agencies' rulemakings to identify other classes of transactions that should be subject to the clearing requirement that had not been submitted to the agency. Section 723(a) of H.R. 4173 (as passed by the Senate).

[18] Section 723(a)(3) of the Dodd-Frank Act (to be codified at 7 U.S.C. §2(h)(3)) (swaps); Section 763(a) of the Dodd-Frank Act (to be codified at 15 U.S.C. § 78a *et seq.*)(security-based swaps).

[19] Section 723(a)(3) of the Dodd-Frank Act (to be codified at 7 U.S.C. §2(h)(8)); Section 763(a) of the Dodd-Frank Act (to be codified at 15 U.S.C. § 78a *et seq.*)(security-based swaps).

[20] Section 723 of the Dodd-Frank Act (new section 5h(e) of the Commodity Exchange Act to be codified after 7 U.S.C. §7b-2).

[21] Only eligible contract participants will be able to trade on SEFs and SBSEFs.

[22] Section 720 of S. 3217, as reported by the Senate Committee on Banking, Housing, and Urban Affairs, Apr. 15, 2010.

[23] Section 720 of the Dodd-Frank Act, P.L. 111-203.

[24] Section 723(a)(3) of the Dodd-Frank Act (to be codified at 7 U.S.C. §2(h)(7)) (swaps); Section 763(a) of the Dodd-Frank Act (to be codified at 15 U.S.C. § 78a et seq.)(security-based swaps).

[25] Id.

[26] The CFTC and SEC must consider whether to exempt small banks, savings associations, farm credit systems institutions, and credit unions from the definition of financial entity in this section. Such a determination could make the end-user exemption available to these entities. Section 723(a)(3) of the Dodd-Frank Act (to be codified at 7 U.S.C. §2(h)(7)) (swaps); Section 763(a) of the Dodd-Frank Act (to be codified at 15 U.S.C. § 78a et seq.)(security-based swaps). (page 822 and 1060).

[27] Sections 3103 and 3203 of H.R. 4173 (as passed by the House).

[28] Sections 723(a) and 763 of H.R. 4173 (as passed by the Senate).

[29] Affiliates of persons qualifying for the end user exception are not eligible to engage in swaps or security-based swaps on the behalf of qualifying persons if the affiliate is a swap dealer, security-based swap dealer, major swap participant, major security-based swap participant, companies that would be investment companies under section 3 of the Investment Company Act of 1940 but for the exceptions provided in subparagraphs (c)(1) or (c)(7) of that section (15 U.S.C. §80a-3), a commodity pool, or a bank holding company with over $50,000,000,000 in consolidated assets. Section 723(a)(3) of the Dodd-Frank Act (to be codified at 7 U.S.C. §2(h)(3)) (swaps); Section 763(a) of the Dodd-Frank Act (to be codified at 15 U.S.C. § 78a et seq.)(security-based swaps).

[30] Section 723(a)(3) of the Dodd-Frank Act (to be codified at 7 U.S.C. §2(h)(4)) (swaps); Section 763(a) of the Dodd-Frank Act (to be codified at 15 U.S.C. § 78a et seq.)(security-based swaps).

[31] Section 723(a)(3) of the Dodd-Frank Act (to be codified at 7 U.S.C. §2(h)(4)) (swaps); Section 763(a) of the Dodd-Frank Act (to be codified at 15 U.S.C. § 78a et seq.)(security-based swaps).

[32] Sections 723(a) and 763 of H.R. 4173 (as passed by the Senate).

[33] Section 723(a)(3) of the Dodd-Frank Act (to be codified at 7 U.S.C. §2(h)(5)).

[34] Section 763(a) of the Dodd-Frank Act (to be codified at 15 U.S.C. § 78a et seq.).

[35] Sections 3103 and 3203 of H.R. 4173 (as passed); Sections 723(a) and 763 of S. 3217 (as passed).

[36] Section 725 of the Dodd-Frank Act (to be codified at 7 U.S.C. §2(a)).

[37] See 15 U.S.C. § 78f.

[38] Section 729 of the Dodd-Frank Act (to be codified at 7 U.S.C. §6o-1) and Section 766 of the Dodd-Frank Act (to be codified at 15 U.S.C. §78a et seq.).

[39] Id.

[40] Section 3101 of H.R. 4173, as passed the House of Representatives, Dec. 11, 2009.

[41] Section 711 of S. 3217, as reported by the Senate Committee on Banking, Housing, and Urban Affairs, Apr. 15, 2010.

[42] This was not a "net" position, and applied to individual categories of swaps, as opposed to the institutions aggregate swaps book.

[43] Remarks of Senator Blanche Lincoln, *Congressional Record*, May 5, 2010, p. S3140.

INDEX

A

abuse, 110
access, 27, 55, 58, 68, 76, 82, 83, 85, 91, 95, 108, 112, 115, 117
accountability, 48
accounting, 52, 69
adverse effects, 12, 13
agencies, 10, 18, 45, 52, 57, 70, 76, 84, 88, 100, 106, 110, 111, 118
agriculture, 3, 46, 50, 101
American International Group (AIG), viii, 73, 75, 78, 92
antitrust, 55
arbitrage, 64
assets, 3, 6, 16, 17, 26, 48, 58, 61, 66, 67, 68, 70, 84, 102, 109, 114, 115, 116, 119
attachment, 94
audit, 30, 55, 108
authority, 10, 11, 25, 30, 40, 41, 43, 46, 47, 48, 51, 52, 53, 55, 57, 58, 70, 73, 74, 76, 77, 83, 86, 87, 105, 110, 117

B

bail, 8, 115
balance sheet, 12, 13, 15, 24, 26, 115
banking, 11, 12, 13, 15, 18, 20, 21, 25, 30, 39, 44, 45, 68, 76, 109, 115
banking industry, 76
bankruptcy, 6, 32, 66, 105
banks, 7, 17, 19, 21, 23, 25, 30, 38, 39, 56, 57, 58, 64, 75, 76, 81, 82, 85, 87, 88, 89, 90, 113, 114, 115, 116, 119
base, 9, 36
benefits, 7, 31, 38, 77, 87
benign, 38
bias, 40
blogs, 28
board members, 86
bond market, 54
bondholders, 62, 63
bonds, 3, 4, 18, 55, 62, 63, 67, 102
breakdown, 65
Britain, 90
business model, 86, 108
businesses, 3, 8, 30, 64, 101
buyer, 60, 61, 64, 65, 67, 69, 70, 71
buyers, 67, 68

C

capital gains, 71
carbon, 51, 52, 73
cash, viii, 2, 6, 21, 46, 59, 63, 64, 65, 67, 68, 69, 70, 71, 72, 75, 77, 100, 101, 108
cash flow, 63, 69, 70, 71
category a, 12, 14
cattle, 31
causal relationship, 41

chaos, 6, 105
Chicago, 70, 71, 88, 91, 95
Chicago Mercantile Exchange, 70, 71, 88, 91, 95
China, 40
City, 95
classes, 8, 33, 34, 92, 118
classification, 49, 66
clearinghouses, viii, 17, 23, 24, 30, 43, 44, 47, 52, 58, 75, 76, 77, 80, 81, 82, 83, 84, 88, 90, 91, 100, 115
coal, 15
collateral, 2, 4, 6, 7, 21, 23, 58, 68, 79, 82, 87, 103, 104
commercial, 12, 13, 15, 16, 19, 23, 24, 25, 26, 30, 31, 33, 41, 48, 49, 50, 54, 65, 67, 69, 76, 80, 81, 86, 87, 100, 109, 110, 112, 114
commercial bank, 76
commodity, vii, 1, 2, 3, 16, 26, 31, 32, 33, 42, 43, 48, 49, 51, 59, 64, 65, 66, 67, 68, 69, 70, 71, 72, 73, 80, 101, 109, 116, 119
commodity futures, 48, 51, 64, 65
Commodity Futures Trading Commission (CFTC), 4, 30, 65, 76, 78, 100, 102
commodity markets, 42
community, 114
competition, 23, 36, 82, 85, 87, 88, 94, 107
complexity, 30, 39
compliance, 6, 79, 104, 108
composition, 86
computing, 36, 67
conference, 83, 84, 116
conflict, 83, 86
conflict of interest, 83, 86
Congress, vii, viii, 1, 2, 7, 27, 29, 30, 31, 36, 40, 41, 43, 47, 48, 52, 54, 55, 56, 75, 76, 77, 80, 81, 83, 92, 93, 99, 116, 117
congressional committees, vii, 29, 31
consensus, 37, 38
consolidation, 36, 37
construction, 3, 102
consulting, 10, 30
Consumer Protection Act, v, vii, 29, 43, 77, 92, 93, 99, 118

consumers, 32
consumption, 32
controversial, 112
convergence, 37
cooling, 65
corporate governance, 90
cost, 23, 36, 37, 51, 53, 62, 113
cost saving, 36
counseling, 68
Court of Appeals, 10
credit market, 7, 68, 101
credit rating, 6, 66, 67, 105
creditors, viii, 99
creditworthiness, 3, 4, 44, 71, 79, 101, 103
crises, 41
criticism, 117
CRS report, 43, 63
crude oil, 15, 33, 39, 41, 72
currency, 9, 61, 62, 63, 66, 67, 68, 69, 71, 96
current limit, 55
customer relations, 18
customers, 3, 33, 44, 53, 64, 67, 68, 92, 101, 107, 108

D

decision-making process, 86
delegates, 48
Delta, 66
depository institutions, 27, 109, 114, 115
deposits, 68, 77, 100
derivatives market, vii, viii, 3, 24, 29, 30, 33, 34, 36, 39, 41, 48, 51, 52, 53, 54, 55, 57, 61, 69, 73, 75, 76, 81, 96, 99, 100, 101, 102, 105, 112
derivatives trading, vii, 3, 23, 29, 31, 39, 40, 41, 42, 43, 77, 96, 101, 108, 115
directors, 86, 90, 94
disclosure, 29, 45, 55
distribution, 1, 7, 39, 101
Dodd-Frank Wall Street Reform, vii, 29, 43, 77, 92, 99, 118
dominance, 88

E

economic fundamentals, 116
economic growth, 38
economic incentives, 81
economies of scale, 36
education, 52
electricity, 15
electronic systems, 108
embargo, 40
emergency, 40, 48, 58, 73, 108
emergency rule, 108
emission, 51, 52
empirical studies, 73
employees, 51, 87
end-users, 23, 30, 54, 100, 109, 113
energy, 3, 7, 30, 32, 38, 40, 41, 42, 43, 45, 46, 48, 50, 51, 52, 65, 67, 73, 101, 116
energy prices, 3, 7, 32, 38, 50, 101
enforcement, 33, 51, 52
engineering, 3, 102
environment, 36, 39, 80
Environmental Protection Agency, 52
equities, 116
equity, 9, 17, 28, 34, 64, 65, 68, 69, 70, 84, 85, 87, 113, 114
equity market, 65
ethanol, 15
ethics, 52
Europe, 50, 51, 88, 90, 91
European Commission, 85, 93
European market, 36
European Parliament, 93
evidence, 40
examinations, 58
exchange rate, 61, 62
exclusion, 24
execution, 18, 19, 20, 64, 67, 88, 89, 91, 93, 100, 107, 108
exercise, 11, 26, 45, 60, 61, 70, 84
expertise, 57, 81, 85, 86, 87, 107
exposure, viii, 12, 13, 23, 24, 69, 75, 76, 77, 78, 81, 87, 100, 101

F

faith, 11
fear, 78, 87
fears, 30
federal agency, 30, 33
federal assistance, 17, 23, 27, 115
federal government, 11
Federal Government, 73, 92
federal law, 33
Federal Register, 93
federal regulators, viii, 29, 45
financial condition, 39, 101
financial crisis, vii, viii, 1, 3, 29, 38, 42, 75, 76, 88, 99, 100, 102
Financial derivatives, vii, 1
financial fragility, 41
financial innovation, 100
financial instability, 81
financial institutions, 1, 5, 8, 30, 32, 36, 39, 45, 55, 57, 76, 79, 83, 84, 100, 101, 104, 112, 114, 115
financial intermediaries, 44
financial markets, 12, 13, 30, 91
financial resources, 77, 81
financial sector, 116
Financial Services Authority, 50, 71
financial shocks, 38
financial stability, 2, 12, 13, 25, 65, 99
financial system, vii, viii, 2, 6, 13, 14, 24, 26, 27, 29, 30, 39, 53, 71, 75, 92, 100, 112, 113, 115
fixed rate, 62, 63, 68, 71
flexibility, 111
fluctuations, 31, 40, 81
force, 80, 87
forecasting, 31, 32
foreign currencies, vii, 1, 67
foreign exchange, 3, 11, 26, 28, 66, 69, 101, 113
formation, 57, 85
fragility, 38, 42
fraud, 33, 44, 52, 53, 55, 69
freezing, 7, 101
fundamental reform, vii, 1

funds, 17, 36, 40, 41, 48, 49, 50, 58, 59, 65, 67, 68, 70, 87, 89, 107, 113, 115, 116

G

gambling, 31
GAO, 51
General Motors, 32
global recession, 40
governance, 76, 80, 82, 83, 84, 86, 87, 90
government credit, viii, 99
government intervention, 2
government securities, 116
grades, 64
Gramm-Leach-Bliley Act, 67
grants, 47, 105
greenhouse, 51, 52
greenhouse gases, 51
growth, 3, 34, 36, 41, 56, 91, 102
guidance, 18, 112
guidelines, 56

H

harmonization, 30
heating oil, 41
hedging, 3, 4, 7, 12, 13, 18, 19, 23, 24, 26, 28, 31, 32, 49, 67, 72, 78, 101, 102, 114, 115
history, 83, 97
holding company, 16, 18, 90, 119
horizontal integration, 91
host, 91
House, 2, 8, 9, 10, 11, 12, 13, 14, 15, 16, 17, 18, 19, 20, 21, 22, 23, 24, 25, 26, 27, 28, 40, 46, 48, 51, 72, 73, 76, 83, 84, 93, 94, 106, 109, 112, 113, 114, 118, 119
House of Representatives, 94, 119
housing, 3, 38, 39, 102
hydrocarbons, 15

I

identity, 44

illusion, 42
image, viii, 75, 100
imbalances, 69
income, 41, 70, 71
increased competition, 36
India, 40
individuals, 89
industries, 67
industry, 40, 54, 57, 69, 70, 76, 80, 87, 88, 90, 95
infrastructure, 36, 53, 107
initiation, 67
insider trading, 47
institutions, 5, 7, 33, 71, 72, 78, 79, 89, 104, 109, 115, 119
integration, 90, 91
integrity, 41, 44, 46, 57, 103, 111
intellectual property, 87
interest rates, vii, 1, 3, 61, 67, 68, 69, 101, 116
intermediaries, 49, 108
International Swaps and Derivatives Association (ISDA), 6, 68, 79, 104
intervention, 100
intrinsic value, 61
investment, 16, 33, 36, 39, 49, 59, 60, 65, 116, 119
investment bank, 33, 49
investments, 87
investors, 33, 36, 37, 40, 41, 47, 49, 50, 64, 67, 68, 87, 95
issues, vii, 2, 10, 48, 78

J

joint ventures, 36
jurisdiction, viii, 29, 30, 45, 47, 48, 56, 57, 105, 106, 110

L

laws, 47, 50, 52, 53, 54, 55, 70, 72
laws and regulations, 50
lead, 30, 81, 85, 88

legislation, 2, 8, 30, 57, 83, 108, 114, 116
legislative proposals, 40
lending, 39, 70
liquid assets, viii, 68, 75
liquidate, 6
liquidity, 3, 7, 40, 46, 58, 69, 82, 101, 106, 115
litigation, 56
livestock, 31
loans, 11, 39, 70, 115

M

majority, 59, 72, 88, 89
management, 13, 14, 24, 58, 86
manipulation, 40, 44, 46, 47, 50, 52, 53, 55, 64, 73, 108, 116, 117
manufactured goods, 12, 16, 110
marginalization, 91
market concentration, 76
market discipline, 38, 53
market economics, 32
market position, 68, 111
market share, 23, 36, 82
market structure, 8, 105
marketing, 55, 68
marketplace, 3, 5, 36, 52, 67, 79, 102, 103
measurement, 67
media, 89, 91, 96
membership, 81, 82, 85
membership criteria, 82
merchandise, 12, 16, 110
mergers, 91
metals, 66, 67, 116
misuse, 86
models, 3, 102
monopoly, 36
mortgage-backed securities, 6, 42, 104

N

national borders, 36
natural gas, 15, 41, 89
New York Stock Exchange, 72, 91

North America, 35

O

Obama, 9, 31, 53, 54
Obama Administration, 9, 31, 53, 54
oil, vii, 29, 34, 38, 40, 47, 48, 49, 59
oil price volatility, vii, 29
operations, 81, 88, 100, 115
opportunities, 42
organize, 91
oversight, viii, 13, 14, 24, 27, 29, 36, 40, 45, 47, 50, 51, 53, 55, 57, 58, 73, 76, 77, 94
over-the-counter (OTC), vii, viii, 1, 3, 29, 30, 75, 76, 95, 99, 100, 102
ownership, 36, 64, 70, 76, 83, 84, 85, 86, 87, 88, 89, 90, 93, 94, 96
ownership structure, 85, 86, 88, 89, 96

P

parallel, 92, 105, 112
participants, 1, 2, 7, 8, 20, 21, 23, 29, 37, 39, 42, 44, 45, 47, 55, 57, 58, 65, 66, 67, 70, 74, 76, 81, 83, 84, 87, 88, 89, 100, 101, 105, 107, 108, 112, 115, 118
permit, vii, 1, 21, 43, 72, 107
Petroleum, 91
platform, 78, 103, 107
police, 53, 55
policy, 35, 82, 87
policymakers, 33
pools, 3, 67, 102
portfolio, 18, 64, 69, 70
President, 47, 73
price changes, 34
price instability, 50
price manipulation, 44, 45, 117
prima facie, 40
principles, 19, 56, 57, 81, 86, 87, 108
probability, 61
producers, 48
professionals, 33
profit, 7, 18, 32, 36, 59, 61, 66, 70, 86

proliferation, 36, 42
propane, 15
protection, 31, 47, 57
prudential regulation, 112, 113
psychology, 32
public interest, 31, 38, 47, 110

risks, vii, 1, 2, 3, 6, 7, 8, 23, 26, 29, 30, 31, 42, 49, 57, 60, 80, 81, 87, 100, 101
root, 55
rules, 10, 14, 21, 24, 33, 46, 47, 49, 50, 52, 56, 67, 70, 73, 76, 83, 84, 85, 86, 87, 88, 90, 92, 94, 108, 110, 111, 117

R

race, 23, 30, 82
rate of return, 64
rating agencies, 66
real estate, 58
real time, 55
recognition, 25
recommendations, 46, 48, 52, 57
reform, vii, viii, 1, 2, 4, 6, 7, 8, 9, 29, 30, 77, 83, 105
Reform, vii, 1, 6, 29, 43, 53, 74, 77, 92, 93, 99, 117, 118
reforms, viii, 43, 57, 75, 78, 81, 100, 103
regulations, 17, 57, 67, 112
regulatory agencies, 72, 87
regulatory changes, vii, 29, 31
regulatory controls, 77
regulatory framework, 53, 86
regulatory oversight, 30, 45
regulatory requirements, 66, 72
relief, 50
renewable energy, 52
rent, 64
repo, 70
requirements, 2, 8, 19, 20, 21, 22, 23, 24, 25, 30, 45, 47, 50, 53, 55, 56, 67, 69, 70, 75, 82, 84, 85, 86, 92, 100, 105, 110, 111, 112, 116
resources, 32, 46, 56, 57, 81, 82, 107, 108
response, 37, 91
restrictions, 83, 85, 86, 88
restructuring, 27, 118
retail, 66, 67
revenue, 71, 87
risk aversion, 35
risk factors, 32
risk management, 30, 38, 58, 80, 82, 87

S

safety, 20, 58, 115
savings, 119
scope, 23, 24, 76, 82, 96
Secretary of Agriculture, 51
securities, 3, 6, 11, 20, 33, 36, 39, 42, 45, 47, 53, 54, 55, 56, 61, 64, 66, 67, 68, 69, 70, 71, 72, 90, 102, 105, 108, 112, 115
Securities and Exchange Commission (SEC), 4, 10, 30, 76, 78, 100, 102
Securities Exchange Act, 11, 55
security, 10, 11, 13, 14, 15, 16, 17, 18, 20, 21, 22, 27, 30, 47, 56, 67, 68, 69, 70, 78, 82, 83, 87, 92, 100, 102, 105, 106, 107, 109, 110, 111, 112, 115, 116, 118, 119
segregation, 67
self-regulation, 44
seller, 32, 60, 65, 67
sellers, 67, 68
Senate, 2, 8, 9, 10, 11, 12, 13, 14, 15, 16, 17, 18, 19, 20, 21, 22, 23, 24, 25, 26, 27, 46, 72, 73, 83, 84, 93, 94, 95, 106, 108, 109, 111, 114, 115, 118, 119
services, 15, 17, 37, 58, 64, 66, 68, 86, 89, 91, 108
shareholders, 89, 90, 95
shock, 26, 38, 42, 101
showing, 49
small businesses, 32
speculation, vii, 1, 31, 38, 40, 42, 45, 46, 47, 48, 49, 52, 60, 73, 116, 117
speech, 38
spin, 23, 115
spot market, 71
stability, 78, 81, 105
stakeholders, 89, 90
standardization, 54

state, 11, 54, 64, 115
states, 11, 22, 55, 90
statistics, 28, 49, 72, 95, 96
statutes, 57
stock options, 4, 35, 102
stock price, 3, 55, 101
stress, 44, 58, 99
structure, 65, 67, 83
subpoena, 52
supervision, 38
supplier, 32
surveillance, 52
survival, 82
systemic risk, viii, 2, 8, 25, 27, 38, 53, 58, 71, 75, 76, 78, 80, 81, 82, 87, 92, 99, 107

T

tactics, 64
takeover, 36, 37, 91
tax breaks, 18
taxpayers, 115
TCC, 96
technology, 36
telephone, 64, 69, 108
terminals, 50
territory, 10
time frame, 40, 59
time periods, 64
Title I, 9, 52, 73, 79, 104
Title II, 9, 52, 73, 79, 104
Title V, 2, 9, 18, 43, 58, 86, 92, 99, 105, 112, 116
trade, 4, 6, 25, 32, 34, 36, 41, 44, 50, 52, 54, 55, 59, 64, 66, 67, 68, 69, 74, 78, 79, 88, 90, 91, 93, 103, 104, 105, 107, 108, 118
trading partners, viii, 99, 100
transaction costs, 60, 91
transactions, 3, 7, 19, 21, 23, 30, 31, 33, 34, 44, 45, 46, 49, 52, 57, 65, 66, 69, 79, 80, 90, 91, 92, 101, 106, 107, 108, 109, 110, 111, 114, 118
transformation, 62
transparency, 2, 29, 30, 38, 53, 54, 55, 57, 82, 105, 107, 108, 117

Treasury, 6, 7, 10, 11, 38, 74, 78, 88, 105
treatment, 11, 48, 107
triggers, 47
turnover, 27, 117

U

U.S. Treasury, 63
UK, 36, 50
uncapitalized exposure, viii, 75, 77, 100
underwriting, 68
uniform, 79
unions, 109, 119
United States (USA), 27, 33, 38, 43, 50, 51, 76, 77, 88, 94, 118
universe, 63

V

variables, vii, 1, 3, 34, 77, 80, 101, 102
variations, 62, 63
vertical integration, 90
volatile commodity prices, vii, 1
volatility, vii, 2, 29, 30, 33, 38, 41, 42, 61, 73, 77, 80, 101, 116
vote, 73, 83, 85
voting, 82, 84, 85, 87
vulnerability, 79

W

Washington, 93
weakness, 99
wealth, 38
web, 1, 39, 74
worldwide, 38, 70
worry, 4, 44, 103

Y

yield, 39